Have We Lost Our Spiritual Connection?

Have We Lost Our Spiritual Connection?

A WAY TO HEAR YOUR INNER VOICE

Written by a Messenger

Clarence L. Brown

ISBN: 1511618558
ISBN 13: 9781511618557
Library of Congress Control Number: 2015905604
CreateSpace Independent Publishing Platform
North Charleston, South Carolina

Table of Contents

Preface

I met Clarence Brown over a decade ago when a friend recommended his acupuncture treatments as a possible determent to neck and shoulder pains I was having. I remember our first meeting and how comfortable I was with his personal mannerisms. He appeared genuinely concerned, without being intrusive. I was mostly impressed with his comprehensive treatment plan. It included explanations of what he would be doing, and the effects of acupuncture on my particular problem areas.

As I had additional treatments and conversations, I became aware of the versatility of Clarence's interests. They ranged from lecturing and leading group discussions to playing the guitar and gardening. He also exemplifies his own health maintenance with biking and tennis, and by keeping abreast of current professional and medical information.

When I first started assisting Clarence with the mechanical aspects of this manuscript I had no idea that the content was so comprehensive. This is not a book to pick up with intent of skimming, or having a "quick read." Rather, it requires an open mind, and the reader's effort to synthesize the content with his/her own background understanding. I found that I had to ponder some of the concepts presented before I could fully assimilate them.

I am honored to be included in the final presentation of this manuscript. The content reflects intensive research from a variety of resources, and encourages eclectic understanding. Readers of this will stimulate their own intellectual curiosity, and will hopefully gain greater insight in responding to the title....<u>Have We Lost Our Spiritual Connection?</u>

Preface By

Chris Christensen

Acknowledgments

I want to say how thankful I am to have been chosen to deliver this message to you. This is a message about recognizing ourselves as spiritual beings and not just as physical bodies.

This message is about <u>love,</u> and our connection to love, which (at its source) is our spirit. My task was to hopefully tell you about how we are all connected at the spiritual level. I hope I have been successful in delivering this message. The idea was to allow us to see that love is always right there in front of us, if we can get out of our way to see it.

I take no credit for the concepts given here in this book. I was spiritually given the topics to explore to help us see the clarity and love these topics can bring forth. To my own amazement I gained proper direction via meditation and observation to bring clarity and understanding to these topics.

You will hear me mention several people that helped me with this project. I am blessed by their patience with me in helping to bring this project alive.

It gives me great pleasure in being able to recognize some of the people that help with the finishing of this project. It has taken me over seven years to complete this manuscript and I could not have been successful without the influence and help of many of these persons.

First and foremost I must thank my parents for allowing me to become the person I am today. But, I think the greatest influence would have to be my older brother, Adell Emerson, who really showed me what love is and what it should feel like.

Also, I thank my late friend and confidante, Annette Lynch, who allowed me to explore many of the ideas at a very early stage of this manuscript. And then, to the little sister I never had, Marsha Emerson, who always believed in me through good and bad times.

I appreciate my sons, Masakela and Ya'Ron Brown, who listened to all of my ideas and gave me their feedback. This has always been a validation of their love to me. Also, thanks to my dearest and oldest friend, Mark Young, who has always been supportive of whatever I chose to do. A special thanks to my friend, Massi Abadi, for her authentic input on an emotional and psycho-dynamic level. Thank you.

A big thanks to my brother, Richard Emerson, for his continued support as I moved along on such a long journey. His positive attitude has kept me focused on the task at hand. Much love Rico, for demonstrating what true <u>love</u> represents… thank you.

When I needed it most God sent me Chris Christensen, my editor and good friend to help me bring the clarity of this material to you he was the person who sat with me week after week to bring forth a comprehensive project. Thank you, I could not have done this without your help. Thanks for being my friend.

I would be remiss if I did not thank a couple of old friends that have been just good supporters of my task in general, Robert Davidson, and Dr. Mark Gerard. Thank you for your endless support over the last twenty years.

CHAPTER 1

How to Touch our Spiritual-Self

I have been searching and pondering for an answer to the question of my spiritual connection for a long time. Never really knowing or understanding what it was, I just continued to search. Back in the late 1980's I started to meditate, to help me understand what it meant to touch my inner-self. So, over the next twenty years, I practiced and grew in my abilities and understanding. After a couple of marriages, and some professional success, I hit a wall. I began to ask, "What next?"

Coming to the end of my second marriage, I started to ask some serious questions about my spiritual-self, as it related to God (our Creator). Not knowing how to approach the topic, I later realized that I could use meditation as a means to discover my spiritual-self. As I started to use this approach I would write down parts of my discovery through meditation. What I soon realized was that many of my brothers and sisters were not conscious of their connection either. This made me wonder if our connection would be universal, and (if so), would we have to follow the universal laws given to us by our Creator. The question is........

Are There Really Coincidences?

"I shall believe that God plays dice with the world"
ALBERT EINSTEIN

It has always been my belief that God created the universal laws, and that there could be no contradiction to these laws. Then, how do we explain synchronicity?

Synchronicity is the experience of two or more events which are causally unrelated, but occur together in a meaningful manner. For synchronous events to occur, they should be unlikely, and must happen by a random chance. This is one of many universal laws that cannot be explained by science or any other means; they just keep showing up in our life. There are far too many of these stories around for us to ignore them.

If we look real closely at the choices we made in our lives, we might easily call them coincidences, because they just appear to happen so randomly. What are some of the synchronous events that we might have experienced? Is it a coincidence that the blind date that you went on led to marriage and or children? What about the unexpected phone call from a friend you had just been thinking about but had not seen for years? Consider that inner-voice that told you not to get on a particular flight, which pulled you away from tragedy. Remember the gift of money that just showed up when you needed it the most! These are just a few examples.

Synchronous events can occur in a large, medium, or small scale. I like to think of the large scale as a <u>major</u> event which is generally seen to affect us long-term. These include marriage, children, jobs, and relationships. All of these can be seen as major synchronous events. <u>Medium</u> events could be like meeting someone today, and months or years later, this connection creates a synchronous event, stemming from that meeting. It is like being in the right place at the right time. It helps us fine tune our course, and keeps us on track. Then there are small reminders or clues which keep us on the correct path. This is like listening to a song and the lyrics tell a story about a question you had been pondering. The author, Squire Rushnell, in his book, <u>When God Winks,</u> calls these clues "guideposts." These are just a few of the clues that keep us on the right path. It is my belief that nothing happens in the universe by accident. So, how could they be accidental?

We are making choices everyday about our direction, and this happens through the process of "free will." These choices influence our reality, which is "our free will." But, behind the scenes, there is something taking place at a higher level. This is why we need the guidance of guides (or spirits) to keep us on our course. When we move with the <u>one</u> <u>direction</u> <u>of</u> <u>love,</u> the path can sometimes appear magical. This is often the moment we recognize that there has been "divine intervention." It is like escaping a fatal accident, or getting the job that you always wanted. The answers just show up, and sometimes totally unexpected. This is what makes synchronous what it is. It is often beyond the self.

My own journey of coincidence started when I was about 11 or 12 years old, when I went to the local swimming pool for the first time. Being from a poor neighborhood, we did not get much supervision about safety around the pool. But that was ok; it was just part of the time in which I grew up.

Not knowing how to swim, I would practice off the end of my bed, and I thought this was enough for me to know about diving into the pool. Well, my big day came, and I went to Lincoln Park for my big swimming day. I went through the process of taking my shower and being checked for the proper height in order for the attendant to allow me to be admitted.

After that inspection, I took off to the pool and (just like the end of my bed) I went head-first in the pool. This landed me at the bottom of the pool, unconscious. The next thing I remember is laying on the side of the pool, as I was looking down at myself. I was quite confused by all this, and wondered how could I be looking down at myself? It all felt so strange, and a few seconds later I was now looking back up at this large crowd of people over me. I was not afraid because I had no idea of what had just happened. It wasn't until later (when I was in the hospital) that it all started to come together. I had just nearly drowned.

As I lay there in the hospital bed looking at the large black clock on the wall, the second hand appeared to stop. I realized that I was replaying my drowning accident and was looking at myself from above. I was very confused by this! So much so that I never told anyone about this for about twenty-five years. Later in my life, I realized that I had an out- of- body experience. Was this just an coincidence or a major turning point in my life?

However, this experience changed my life, because I started to look outside-the-box on most everything I saw. I did not learn how to swim, because I did not return to the pool. However, the universe provided me with many other things to keep life interesting. I went on to become a dad, a business man, a doctor of Oriental Medicine, and now a messenger for this book.

Making The Connection

I delivered newspapers around my neighborhood, and I always passed a small building. One day, I went into the building to see if I could get another customer. But, instead, I had one of those magical moments. I met one of those spiritual guides, one of those persons who turns your life around. This "guide" influenced my thoughts in new ways, giving me a new direction of looking at things. This type of meeting is never just a coincidence. It is a gift to our spiritual connection. These influences help us stay connected by allowing us to realize we are not alone.

This guide was Mrs. Brown. She was a local business woman in the neighborhood where I grew up and she became my mentor and my best friend. Mrs. Brown's mentoring helped me a lot; far more than I could have then imagined. In the late 1950's it was quite uncommon for a black kid and a white woman to be best of friends. But, in our own small way, we were making a statement about real love, and about our connection.

We would talk about everything, and no subjects were off limits. From our first encounter I realized that I was being given a precious gift of life! Later that year, I realized that Mrs. Brown and I had <u>many</u> things in common.

Not only did we have the same last name, but several other things. She told me that she was four-feet -eleven inches tall, and I had learned several weeks before that I also was four-feet-eleven inches tall. My weight was ninety- nine pounds, and so was Mrs. Brown's.

Several months had passed by now, and it was coming near my birthday. To my amazement, I learned that Mrs. Brown's birthdate was also the same as mine, November 20 (although the year was different). I thought that all these coincidences were crazy; all these special things were continuing to show me that we were truly connected. And now, I understand that we were supposed to meet. And this was not just a coincidence—but a spiritual connection!

Here again, the universe was giving me my guide, to help me understand what it is like to have a big sister, or an aunt that is not part of my blood family. However I felt her closeness as being very much a part of my family.

After a short time, we became inseparable. She continued to show me many things in her printing business. The irony is that some thirty-five years later I became quite successful in the printing business, as a salesman with a company called Veron Corporation (a Los Angeles based printing company).

As I look back, I wonder if these events or circumstances were just coincidences, or, are they really just miracles being revealed. There has always been a continuous flow of energy between us all, allowing us to have a whole array of experiences. This was one of those times for me; I experienced family and love, from a whole different level.

Mrs. Brown had become a part of my family because of our sharing of love. This is one of life's most fundamental laws of attraction, which makes family what it is.

Joe Hersh (my next door neighbor when I was a kid) was a tall German who always listened to Beethoven or Bach or some other classical piece of music. I always asked him why he wanted to listen to such boring music! Being only 9 or 10 at the time (and growing up on rock-n-roll or R & B music), I could not understand why he wanted to listen to that kind of music. Joe explained to me that it was relaxing and soothing to his spirit. I responded that as a kid I didn't need to relax. Then he said that I needed the exposure, and asked me to listen, and so I did. Some forty years later, I am quite a lover of the classics, so much so that I have taken up classical guitar.

According to Squire Rushnell in his book, <u>When God Winks,</u> he called these experiences "signposts." Whether we are conscious of it or not, we are all given guides to help us navigate any problem or circumstance that we may face. We must be willing to surrender to our spirits or guides in order to hear this inner-voice! This is one way to make our connection.

Polarities

I have often pondered the idea of <u>polarity</u>. Polarity can be many different things; it can be the positive and negative poles that keep the planet in orbit, or the difference between left and right, or top and bottom. Polarity is to acknowledge the opposite side of what we are seeing or experiencing at any particular moment. It allows us to look for clarity and a clear perception of that moment. Polarity could also represent a break in our spiritual connection, which allows us to see only a <u>partial</u> <u>view.</u> But with this partial view, we can not define the whole; it only provides a limited understanding of what just took place. So, before we move forward we must ask for clarity about a partial view!

The clarity comes when we recognize that we are <u>special</u>, and that the polarity is just a part of the whole. The "special" we are talking about is not for the ways we look, or the things we have or don't have. Special is to recognize the connection we have with our spiritual self ——and our connection to other beings. We must find peace in the fact that special does not live outside of us, and that it always comes from within.

We will never be able to touch our spiritual self if we seek our happiness or peace from outside of ourselves. Unfortunately, there are too many of us that don't believe that they are special. We often seek validation of this in the things we own, or the house we live in, or the goals we have accomplished. The tragedy is that many times we fail to understand that these are meaningless, without happiness. So, the real question we need to ask ourselves is—— can we be truly happy with just our material things?

Society has persuaded us to believe that these material things are extremely important, and that we must have them. However, if we accept this <u>partial view</u>, it will only lead to confusion, and this will make us fearful and doubtful of ourselves. This will make us question the specialness that resides within us all. Then, we will not be able to know our own clarity (in that true knowing is beyond our perception) and our clarity is always right in front of us. If we allow our fears and doubts to rule us, then life's excitement will then fade and pass us by! Fear and confusion will always produce a feeling of lack or weakness, reflecting its own polarity and a partial view.

When fear takes over our lives, we will only be able to focus on the partial-view. There is little that can be revealed from this viewpoint. If we continue to doubt ourselves and our love of self, we will <u>not</u> be able to touch our spirit. We will not be able to see our wholeness, and we will then be left to believe that the partial view is all there is.

This is what is meant by denying the clarity we see; never being able to know the whole. We thus lose our spiritual connection, and the connection to our brothers and sisters. This denial will lead to feelings of suspicion and mistrust, and will continue to have us harbor doubt and confusion within us. This comes about when we function with only a partial-view. With this approach, we cannot see the whole of us, and we become trapped by the <u>polarity</u> of only a partial-view. It is important to take a closer look at why we believe that a partial-view is acceptable.

Spiritual-Self

Have you ever wondered if you had a spiritual-self, and what does that really mean? Does that make you want to ask the question:

Am I greater than what my eyes show me in the mirror? If so, what is it that you see? Most of us do not ponder this thought very much. The thought that we are greater than what is shown to us brings on doubt and fear that we cannot bear. I don't know if that is good or bad. It is not for me to judge, but for me to encourage you to look deeper inside yourself for a better understanding of yourself. Do all of us have a spiritual connection? The answer is" Yes." This is our inherent gift, given to all of us! It is given to us by God (our Creator), for us to know that we are all the same in spirit and that our appearances only reflect a small part of the whole. We are <u>not</u> taught this, but we need to understand this before we can make our spiritual connection.

Do you have someone that you are really close to, that you don't see on a regular basis? But you talk to others about this person quite often, even though you don't see them regularly. But when you do see them, it always feels like it was just yesterday that you saw them last. This is about feeling connected. Another example of this is when you meet someone for the first time and you feel like you have known them for years. This is about the spiritual connection and how it removes time and space from the equation.

Have you ever decided to phone someone, and at the very moment you pick up the phone, they say hello to you? I am not talking about looking at your phone ID. Is this just a coincidence, or is this a spiritual connection? Wouldn't you think that the spiritual connection of <u>love</u> –is outside the scope of coincidences?

Can true love ever be an accident, or something we created? I have always thought that love was <u>to be revealed</u>, <u>rather than created</u>. My friend Nettie says that love "*just Is,*" and is always there; <u>it just needs to be recognized</u>. Let us ponder this for a moment.

Have you ever been in the parking lot at a supermarket, and observed an old lady struggling to put a large box in her car? You rushed to help her, and because of this you felt like someone had just given you a great gift for your act of kindness. Even though the gesture was small one, it lifted the spirit of your heart, and it left a positive impression. The good feeling of helping is what love is all about– the act of sharing oneself.

Another example of this connected love might be when you witness a major accident (where perhaps even a life was lost) and you felt sorrow in your heart, even though you did not know the people involved. You experienced a sense of loss and pain, as if you were a part of the accident scene. This is what tells us we are all connected, and part of the total integration of all living beings.

So why do we often struggle with having a spiritual connection? Why is it so hard to believe in the spiritual part of ourselves? Perhaps this doubt comes from our conditioning. We are so accustomed to believing that "special" comes from good deeds or acts of kindness, and not from the love within.

Our conditioning tells us that good deeds come from outside of us. This kind of projection creates a need for rewards and praise, which satisfies our feeling of being in control. But this shows little to express our willingness to share our love. These emotional and behavioral needs are but a process of personal gratification, which holds us captive to the belief that our conditioning and patterns are who we are.

The truth of the matter is that feeling happy only requires our willingness to be present —and that is all! The spiritual connection can only reflect the clarity, which is right in front of us. The person that laughs a lot finds it hard to be sad, for joy and sadness do <u>not</u> go together. We must recognize there is always a choice to be made to have a connection.

Faith

To connect to our spirit, we must be willing to have faith. Our Holy Spirit is the essence of faith, and this force can only be felt, not seen. Faith is beyond conditioning, and will always allow us to see the Truth. There is nothing we need to do, but to be willing to receive. The key to receiving is in our willingness to surrender and have our arms and our hearts wide open. This is an implicit gift, given to all of us as a means to be connected. There is only one emphatic Truth. It holds true for everyone, regardless of religion, economic position, or social status in life.

This gift must come from <u>beyond</u> the gift of mankind. We need to acknowledge that the Truth is more than a word, or a criterion to be evaluated. The human race is trapped by its own conditioning. Until we can see beyond our own conditioning, we will not recognize true love. It is imperative for us to accept our love of self, in order to make our spiritual connection, and to have faith. We must be willing to question what our eyes show us, so that we may evaluate it for its Truth. Truth is never abstract or hidden. It is always obvious; this is God's gift and promise to all of us. It will always be present, and right in front of us.

This could only be true if it is a part of us, at our core foundation. Then, all that is necessary is for us to recognize that <u>we</u> do <u>not</u> make the Truth! It is outside, or beyond our control, for **_Truth just is!_**

Recognizing Our Godliness

This means that we are something <u>greater</u> than our physical self, as we know it. It is hard for us to phantom (or to believe in our connection) in a Godly way. We must become aware of our inner-self, in order to recognize that part of us, which is eternal. This universal Truth lies within all of us. By looking inwardly for this Truth, we allow ourselves to not feel the pressures of life and the external forces that it can apply.

"Our Godliness" has been called many things over the years, by many different cultures. However, its primary purpose (in most of these cultures) was to allow the individual to know his true value, and to connect to his oneness within. But over time, we have lost the connection to our godly understanding and to our spiritual self.

The pressure of society has smothered the flame of our spirit, to such a point that we no longer believe that we are **"Godly!"** We have become afraid of speaking of ourselves as **Godly**. This continuous denial of our universal gift (being Godly), has left us bewildered in our beliefs, and hinders our willingness to love. This has caused a continuous conflict within us and also within our brothers and sisters, as well. If we can not trust the oneness in ourselves, we will not be able to trust it in others. So, we become even more confused by what we feel in our own hearts. In our confused state, we ultimately make these pressures enormous. These pressures are found in our jobs, our marriages, our relationships, and in our religions. We have given away our freedom by allowing these pressures to become greater than the *essence of our being*.

Our Godly Intent

We need to learn how to refocus our energy to look inside our being, in order to reconnect to our godly self. Then, we will be able to expresses our true ***intent of heart***. The idea of intent of heart speaks to the direction of our true intent; not the one we speak about but the one we perform. It is one that tells us what we are doing and why we are doing it. I believe we can all agree that the outcome of any event can only be predicted with small level of certainty. However, our actions can always be directed by our own intent of heart. Ask yourself the question, "Do I do Godly things every day?"

Most of the people that I spoke with started out by saying "no," they do not perform Godly acts on a daily basis. But after a short conversation with them on the subject, they started to realize that, "yes they do" perform these subtle acts of kindness and clarity every day. In the book, A Course in Miracles, it states that clarity is but a miracle being revealed.

What are some of these godly acts? To answer that question we must first understand that society's conditioning and pressure are the driving forces behind our not recognizing our godliness. It is our choice to choose what we have made! Yes, it is our choice to make! To not allow ourselves to feel the pressure or stress in our everyday lives, is, indeed "Godly." Yes, Just making this thought of this is "Godly"!

Participating in an event, and not feeling a part of it, is almost impossible. However, if you were a part of the event, you had to receive it on some level. For example, you needed a doctor on a Saturday morning and you just showed up completely unannounced at his office. And he greeted you with a level of anticipation. Some would call this a coincidence or just luck. But he had to accept his participation on some level for the event to take place. I recognize this as being connected in a united way, and this connection is <u>always</u> guiding us to the right place, at the right time. This is an example of a "godly act" which is a reflection of love and union, and our true intent of heart.

Spirituality is to be a connection to the soul or spirit, and is considered to be a higher part of our minds. It shows us a refinement in our thought-system. With this refinement we can have a better clarity of thought. We all come with a <u>spiritual connection</u> as a part of our birth right! This creates an automatic connection to our inner-self that creates the joining of the minds of all people of the world. Spiritual connection is beyond words. There is a union about the connection that words can<u>not</u> explain.

While talking with some friends about their communication with their infant, I gained a new understanding of the connection, on a different level. Even though their baby did not have the ability to speak with words, they were still able to know and understand what their baby's needs were. This is a common experience among most parents; they have this intuitive understanding with their child. Children all over the world are able to let their parents know their needs at any moment in time. They communicate with a common voice. They speak with the universal voice of our <u>spiritual connection</u>—which is given at birth, to all of us. Some parents find it easy to communicate this way, and others find it quite difficult.

Why is that? Perhaps, it is because some parents function with the thought-system of <u>love</u>, while others expresses a thought-system of <u>fear</u> and confusion. We must choose only one of these two thought-systems that are available to us. However, we cannot choose both without creating confusion and doubt. To believe we can possess both is to choose fear as our ally. An example of this would be how some parents interpret changing a soiled diaper. Some will view this as a sacrifice; other as a reflection of love, and good health. It's just that simple of a choice! We can all learn to communicate on a totally different level if we are willing to make a spiritual connection. But, the bigger question is," Are we willing to make the connection?"

Recognizing Our Blessings?

To see our blessings, we must allow ourselves to recognize that we are blessed—in our own way. Generally speaking, when we start to pass judgment on a particular outcome or event we are asking for trouble. This implies that we had an expectation going in and knew already what we wanted as the outcome. This approach will often cloud our perception, about the actual outcome. It allows us to create an outcome that we would like to see, rather than accepting the one that has already happened. This will usually leave us confused about how to accept the reality of what <u>did</u> happen. This, in turn, will promote the need for us to create our own conclusions. We are <u>now</u> in our own way (with our projections about tomorrow) and with our view of the way things should be.

So how do we really know what has already happened? Like I stated before, to get out of our own way, we must learn to love ourselves! If we can surrender to the spiritual part of us, we will realize that we do not have to do anything, because love is given to us.

Our reality is only influenced by us, but it is not created by us. We often like to think that reality needs a little more from us; so, we add our input, trying to make it better. Think of it this way: loving ourselves is like playing a sport, or playing an instrument. The more we do it, the easier it becomes. Thus, learning becomes natural, and is not created.

Our part is to recognize that we are always at the right place at the right time, and we must be at peace with where that is! Then, we will begin to receive the greatest of all blessings—self-love.

Athletes in many different sports have spoken of being "in the zone." This is not an energy or a place that you can conjure up when you want to. The process does not work that way. But, on any particular day, everything can fall into place, and you can find yourself "in the zone." The ball will appear to be moving in slow motion in tennis; the notes appear to light up in your mind's eye on the guitar; a runner feels as though he is floating over the surface of the track. Each of us needs to learn how to get out of our way......"to feel the zone." The zone is always there, but it is hindered by our own internal conflicts and denials. We often deny ourselves the whole view, only to accept what <u>we</u> <u>wanted</u> to see. I think this happens to a lot of us, because we have accepted a belief-system that no longer allows us the ability to recognize our blessing.

We are driven by the consistent patterns and frequencies of our belief-system regardless of what it is that we are doing. When we can let go, and learn to use the natural approach to our growth, things get easier. For example, the swimmer that has a smooth stroke recognizes how much faster he can go. However, the connection requires him to let go to find the zone. What I am speaking about is the idea of surrendering to the connection; then, everything else will take care of itself! Then we can recognize our blessings.

There is no reason for this perfect behavior, it is about trusting the natural way of learning. If you have become really good at something you had to surrender to it in order to receive the blessings. When we have learned to surrender our blessings will happen naturally. Most animals learn in this natural way, but our human egos have convinced us otherwise. We believe it, so we can be in control, thus, making it what we want. But when we use this approach we lose the connection to the zone, and that is the unfortunate result. The zone doesn't need our input to be what it is.

We must appreciate that we do not have to be perfect, but only to allow ourselves to observe perfection. By experiencing perfection, we only have to realize what happened, or to acknowledge what we have taken in. Then, we must look at what went wrong to evaluate the blessing of our original plan. By understanding what went wrong we will know what happened, as long as we don't alter or judge the outcome. This could very well be an outcome that we did not want.

So, when we slow down and look at the old plan, we realize (at that moment) our heart is no longer filled with anger and frustration. We can then look to the possibilities of growth, and to the excitement of surrendering to our blessings.

Self-love is not that hard to obtain if we allow ourselves to get out of our own way. Whatever we do must be done from the right mind-set and with a pure intent of heart. This is imperative to our connection if our union is to be maintained.

Self-Love

The key to recognizing self-love is to realize what it is that we think we know. We often believe that it is all about what is in our head, rather than what is in our intent of heart. We need to slow down to feel this experience! If we move too fast, we will only get a glimpse of the experience, and, with it, only a partial view. We must recognize that the experience is our blessing. However, we must first be ready to receive it, to know it in its totality, and to know that the experience is never partial. But, this requires us to be willing to receive the whole experience. A great example of this might refer to musicians or athletes who are able to find "the zone." Thereby, they allow themselves a chance to experience the whole, and <u>not</u> just that small glimpse. This can only happen when we are able to "get out of our way." If we can do this (get out of our way), we can experience more than we could ever have imagined.

To feel the love of our sons or daughters, wives or mothers, or just good friends, we must be willing to experience the love as it is, which requires a <u>union</u> or a <u>connection</u>. The process is to look at the event that is right in front of us, and <u>not</u> the one we wanted to be there—but the one that is there.

Anger, fear, and frustration (along with anxiety) are all expectations of an outcome we want to happen, but did not happen. These are but projections of our inner-fear, and confusion of a pending outcome. When we see this rage of conflict and confusion in our brother's or sister's faces, it is because we have seen this same conflict in our own face and heart. This rage and conflict are what we need to process, because this is what makes us fearful. These emotions and behavior of rage have no power of their own. We must recognize the source of this confusion and rage, and learn how not to project it. We need to realize that its power is coming from within us.

How many times have you been in a conflicting scenario, but did not_allow yourself to become enraged by the heat of the moment? Usually, after a short time the other party will follow our lead and calmer heads will prevail. This requires us to stay centered and to take it all in, both the good and bad. We need to see both sides in order to have the whole picture. To endure the rage of the moment (it won't kill you), try to be patient with your brothers. If we can exercise this kind of patience we will see that it is worth its weight in gold! We all want to be happy and loved, and patience is one of the ways to find it.

I think we have all heard the phrase, _stay in the moment._ This implies patience and focus. However, to accomplish this also implies a stagnant moment, rather than a dynamic one. This phrase, (stay in the moment) could be quite confusing. In considering "the moment" we must consider that nature is always fleeting, and cannot be static. But, if we believe that we <u>can</u> stay in the moment, we will have to believe that we can deny the natural laws of nature. This could only further confuse us as to who we believe we are. So, how could this ever be a loving approach to ourselves?

When I ask this question of most people, whether they love themselves or not, it is very interesting to hear their replies. The immediate response is yes, sure, absolutely, "of course I love myself." But when we carried the conversation on for a while, they will start to recant their response in some ways. Because, unfortunately, a lot of us do <u>not</u> give ourselves much love. If we look around us, we may see just the opposite. We can be quite harsh and cruel to ourselves.

Then, it stands to reason why it would be so hard to give this love away, when we do not have it, or possess it, for ourselves. Love, unlike most things, cannot be packaged or wrapped to be given away. It requires our connection and our presence; and for that, we must be present! This means that we must surrender and listen to that inner-voice of love that moves only in one direction. So, we must recognize our love within us, in order to share it with others. Remember, love needs only our presence to exist!

Our Conditioning

Conditioning is a very important idea to discuss. Most of the things we do and talk about come to us by some means of data passed on by our society or culture. According to Wikipedia, social conditioning refers generally to societal and political mechanisms or processes that regulate individual and group behavior. This often leads to conformity and compliance to the rules given by the society, state, or social group.

Our conditioning can be an important part of our social control in that it is part of an individual's socialization process. Most societies have universal norms or rules which should be followed by members of that society. However, to deviate from these norms could result in punishment by the social order. This Sociological process of training individuals leads to conformity. The manifestations of social conditioning are vast.

There are two social-control mechanisms used either through formal or informal means. Formal social control is expressed through laws and statutes, or rules and regulations against deviant behavior. In democratic societies, the goals and mechanisms of formal social control are determined through legislation by elected representatives. These elected persons enjoy a measure of support and voluntary compliance from the population. A law against deviant social behavior, such as murder, is directed at all members of society. Fishing and hunting regulations are for certain groups. Formal control is conducted by government, and organizations, through law enforcement mechanisms.

Informal social control is an exercise by a society without the use of stated rules or laws. They are generally expressed by norms and customs. These may include shame, criticism, ridicule, or disapproval from a teacher for a student being out of line. Informal control is effective in small group settings, including family, neighborhood, or work places just to name a few.

The essence of social control can be traced back to how it has influenced us for many years. This can determine how we see and treat our brothers and sisters; determine what their values are, and what is important to them. While the focus is all on the individual, the values are all coming from the outside. Where there is no connection, how can there be real value in such a vague approach? Things do not just happen by a means of chaos, but more often, they are influenced by a state of chaos, in a very calculated way. This is why the peer group within a society (the ones who make the rules and create the norm), is able to shape the way we think, and influence our behavior.

Questioning Our Conformity

We must start to question our conditioning, because most of the information given to us to make our decisions (about our ethical, social, and economic issues) are flawed. But, this is the nature of conditioning: to serve a few, and confuse the others. This approach is all about separation—not joining!

The separated mind can only maintain its separation, except by the means of disassociating with others.

If we chose to look for love outside of ourselves, perhaps we are not looking for true love, but merely for a response to the idea of love. When we look at this closely, we will see that a response only continues the conversation; but it does not leave us with any level of clarity or understanding. Before we go on, let's look at the many faces of conditioning.

We must first look to our parents and to our society. They both carry a broad level of influence on our behavior, primarily in our early years. It was stated earlier that social influences and conditioning are passed on by our society, teachers, etc., and have created the need for us to want to be a part of a particular group. This conditioning has led us to be afraid of ourselves, and our brothers. This misinformation approach (given to us by society) has produced a level of separation and confusion within us all.

This process of conditioning began with our parents, who actually started with the deck stacked against them. Because they, too, were conditioned by their parents, so they merely passed on old social dogma, and just believed what they were told. But, they seldom allowed themselves to question their history. Think of all the things we do every day, because it was the way that our dad did it; or that was the way my grandma made it.

This is not about the right or wrong, or the good or bad of their teaching, However, it does require, *that we question it.* When we start to question our conformity, and look at our actions, do we find the happiness we seek? Do our actions reflect our love? We are the only ones who really know our true intent of heart. And this will always reflect the true purpose of our actions.

I remember when I was about 12 years old, and my dad wanted me to go to the lumber yard with him to read over a contract that he was entering into with the lumberyard owner. I was excited to go and help my dad with a business matter. My dad told me to wait in the car until he called for me. He walked around the yard showing the owner what he was going to need for our new house project. They stood at the front of the yard near the car, where I was waiting for my signal to come and help. I thought it is now going to be my turn, in just one more minute. As my excitement grew, I looked up and saw my dad giving his hand to the other man in a gesture of good will. Moments later, my dad returned to the car. I asked what happened, "Dad didn't you need my help to read the contact." He replied, "Son, did you see me give my hand to that man?" I replied, "Yes, sir."

Then he went on to tell me what he meant. He told me that he had <u>nothing greater</u> than his word, and that his hand shake was going to be his contract. It took me many years, before I really understood my dad's wise advice and his gift to me. To this day, I have never forgotten that experience, or those words of wisdom. But, it was in my questioning his gift, which allowed me to understand my dad's actions, and my willingness to follow his wise words. This allowed me to be truthfully guided by my own <u>intent</u> <u>of</u> <u>heart</u> and to my own spiritual connection.

The greater part of us is our internal "word" that allows us to bring value to ourselves and to others. This speaks to the Truth, which we carry within us. However, for some of us, we choose not to recognize it and <u>not</u> to allow ourselves to see the love that is within us. If we cannot see this truth in ourselves we will not recognize it in others. This will breed suspiciousness and mistrust. When we tell someone what we are going to do, no one else made that statement but us. It is important that we understand our own intent of heart by questioning the statements we make!

Society has impacted us in so many different ways, and this impact has made it hard to know the right direction to choose. We have been lead, told, guided, directed, pushed, and manipulated to go a particular direction. The unfortunate part is that we have accepted what we have been told for so long, that we find it hard to step out of the line of conformity. So, we have accepted conformity as safe and comfortable. And yet, we continue to follow the group, even though on some level we believe that they are wrong.

This mode of conditioning comes from our parents, teachers, and our cultures. The impact of this process has been enormous! It has influenced us in so many different ways, and has come from so many different sources, which has made it is hard to stop!   But, this is why we must question our conditioning.

Faith In Our Tomorrow

If we are not allowing ourselves to experience the moment, then how can we ever understand that moment? When we deny ourselves the opportunity to experience the moment, we find ourselves living in the past, or trapped by the thoughts of tomorrow. Neither our thoughts of the past, or our projections into the future, will allow us to experience today. And, yes, we can choose a direction that is wrong sometimes, and even painful. But we must understand that it is only hard to accept because we have been told over and over for years to do it a particular way.

To question our choices and guidance, and to go out on the limb (of life), can be fearful. To go against what we have been taught for years can be quite upsetting. But to it is imperative that we have faith in ourselves, to allow our Spiritual-Self the opportunity to experience that moment. With this step of faith, we will be able to recognize the Truth and <u>not</u> try to create one. This is what faith is all about. The willingness to see what is in front of us gives us a chance to experience it (without controls). This will be one of the biggest steps we will ever take. Our societies have always told us "what to do," and "how to do it," and that made us believe we were in control.

But, the truth of the matter is, we have very little control. It is important that we understand this because we really do <u>not</u> have much control. Remember, society's rules or controls only bring about a temporary fix. We are never told that the rules or laws are not to be a long-term solution. All we need to do is just look around us to clarify this statement! Did these solutions of society bring on any permanence or long-term changes of peace and love in our lives?

The constant bombardment (by all these outside sources) has brought about who we really think we are——and it has been very convincing! And yet, when we look closely, there is nothing concrete about the answers from these outside sources. Truth is not only expressed in words. However, it is also important that they are verified by our actions. This is why it is so important that we experience what is in front of us, because this is verifiable. Anything else is something that can be created or constructed, which may or may not be real.

Do Our Actions Reflect Our Direction?

Our actions reflect the Truth, and our purpose reflects our intent of heart. Then, our Purpose is always led by thoughts, and our actions produce our results. Have you ever had a friend tell you that they would be there for you in a moment of crisis? But, when the chips were down, they were nowhere to be found. There are no words that carry <u>intent</u> without action! The words that we deliver should always come from that place of love. If we can do this, our intent would have but <u>one</u> <u>direction</u>, and that intent would be filled with love! But if our intent is filled with confusion and fear, how would we expect love to be the outcome from such a poor source?

There is <u>no</u> spiritual intent behind any words or actions that do not lead with the purpose of love at its core. Love always brings about a "we" action, and this helps us realize that we are not alone (and have never been alone). Thus, it allows us to see the union, in our oneness. However, this requires faith. We must question or search our connection to see if we are walking with faith and peace in our hearts. Then we will know if our actions are a reflection of our direction.

Recognizing Our Unity

By recognizing our unity we can see our <u>oneness,</u> and there is no need to be afraid or to be confused. Our sameness cannot be different; so, there can be no conflict. This does not mean the sameness in our physical appearance, but rather in our spiritual being. This means that our spirits are far more than the limitations of our physical body. This is very important for us to understand.

Peace comes to us through our clarity and understanding, which is (and has always been) with us. However, we might not have realized its presence. Our body is but a medium for us to communicate with others and to share life's experiences. These experiences allow us to recognize how we are united. This unity allows us to look at one another, and see our physical differences. And yet, we see beyond the body to our union and oneness as a spiritual being. This speaks to the compassion and love that comes from clarity and understanding.

Why Are We So Divided?

Separation is a major player in how we see our brothers and sisters of the world. How we choose to perceive them is what we will see within ourselves. If we have determined that they are different and separate from us, we will not seek a union with them. So, if we maintain our focus upon this division or separation, we will become confused. And if we accept this confusion, we have also made a choice of our belief system and our direction.

If we have accepted the influences of our social system and culture, it tells us to conform to a particular mode of thinking.

This will, then, give us a justification for our actions and suspicions. We are but a small part of the universe, but a most important part. We were all given the ability to recognize our Godliness, and the Godliness of our brothers and sisters, as well. Failing to recognize our spiritual self is like asking the universe to give us something to be different and separate. This would require us to deny the one universe we have right in front of us.

This has been perpetuated by many societies and cultures through conditioning, and it continues to be a problem, even to this day. We must understand the social influences of our times, and how they impact our lives. Until we recognize the conditioning of our times, we will always struggle with finding our own peace and union. This struggle results from the feeling of being lost and divided.

CHAPTER 2
Feeling Lost and Alone

In talking about <u>being</u> <u>lost</u> we have to look at how we see and look at time itself. If we are seeing time as a chronicle of our past, wouldn't that mean that we consistently bring forward the past to meet the future and overlook the present? With this process it does not allows us to consider the <u>present</u>, only the past and the future. If we are to take the past and project it into the future, we would have to keep the idea of the past alive. How often have we met someone new, who looked, talked, walked and acted like someone else from our past? And this brought up all those old bad memories and feelings about our past. However, the other person had no idea why we were acting so weird. We have brought all that bad information or negative energy from the past into our new experience. This floods our thoughts about this new person we have just met. We brought the past to the present without ever realizing it. This is what I am calling, being lost.

We are often not willing to look at the <u>present</u>, or <u>now</u>, and yet this is where our blessings are, and where real change takes place in the <u>now</u>! We have negated the present in our lives by our desires to hold on to yesterday, and make it real. We must be patient with ourselves to allow peace to help us to be aware of the now. This allows us time to experience the moment, and to recognize this is where peace resides. To recognize "now" is the only place where joy and happiness can be found, and where we no longer feel lost or alone. It is important to realize the past is gone, and the future has not arrived. If we attach the past and the future to our "now" we will make it an illusion and <u>not</u> real. We must allow ourselves a chance to experience the events and not judge it by yesterday——— merely let them be what they are. We must recognize that yesterday is gone and can never be duplicated!

Being Lost

Being lost is wanting to believe or to try and make the past and future come together as a continuous process, with no time to evaluate the now. Sigmund Freud introduced this as the "Alter-Ego," as a means to focus our misunderstanding on the irrational thoughts we bring forth. The word *Ego* is taken from Latin, and is translated as "I myself" or to express emphasis. The Latin term *ego* is used in English language to translate Freud's German term (Das Ich) which literally means "the I." However, in modern day society, the ego has many meanings. It could mean one's self-esteem, or an inflated sense of self-worth, or (in philosophical terms) one's self as in spiritual awaking. Originally, Freud had associated the word "ego" to meaning a sense of self. However, he later revised it to mean a set of psychic functions such, as judgment, tolerance, control, intellectual functioning and memory.

In so doing, he gave room for the continuous doubt about who we are and how we function. Here, again, is another way for us to see ourselves as lost. The ego's function is to have us think of the things we made, and label them as our creations. These things are what we have made valuable. At the same time, the ego wants to keep us confused over what it all means, and how it is to be interpreted and valued. So, by the ego's design, we must be kept in the dark, and out of touch with the present. This will keep us confused and feeling lost about who we are. This method or thought-system has been perpetuated over the years by most societies *at all cost.*

If the energy of our ego keeps us dwelling on what happened yesterday, last week, or last year, we will have to bring those thoughts to the forefront of our consciousness. Thus this allows us to dwell in the past, which gives us little chance to evaluate who and where we are now. If we did not take the time to process these bad experiences, they will linger and make us feel trapped. Time, by our own request, has held that experience right where we wanted it, in the past. But when we move from the past to the future, without a conscious understanding of the present, how could we not feel confused and lost?

This will have us deny the blessing of *our present*. How can we ever experience anything, if we are not willing to receive it in the first place? To be a receiver, we must be willing to open up our hearts, to let the experience in.

When we do not allow ourselves to experience of the "now," we have moved time straight from the past to the future. Only in the <u>now</u> can we experience our blessings. Blessings can only be experienced in reality—— and reality is all about the now! This is the only proper use of time. This is what I believe Freud was saying in psychoanalysis, by having us look at the confusion and our egocentric approach of how we see ourselves. A way to no longer feel alone or lost.

Following Their Lead

We have been told all of our lives who we are, and there have been many different versions of who we believe we are, whether that message is delivered by our parent, teacher, priest, or society in general. We have become quite confused over who we are, and about what is real. Through our ancestral teachings, we have come to trust yesterday's information as though it were today's news. We have accepted this new experience and information which came bearing the blessings of truth.

Look at how often we have heard our parents tell us about how their parents looked at a particular subject. Then they would insist that we do it, the same way. Our parents have always told us what to do and how to do it, ever since we were children. We accepted that our parents were just passing on information. However, we never understood that they never really fully understood the information for themselves.

Franz Boas (the father of anthropology in the United States), studied immigrant children to demonstrate that biological race was not immutable, and that human conduct and behavior resulted more from <u>nurture</u> rather than <u>nature</u>. This implies that our behavior patterns that we were given as children have taught us to behave in a particular way. However, if their data is not accurate, they are just passing on poor perceptions and bad information, creating bad behavior patterns.

A New Way Of Thinking

In looking for a new way of thinking about ourselves, we must first have the courage to ask some simple questions, (but critical ones) about our lives. Questions like: What does peace and joy really mean for us? Is peace and joy a part of the natural course of things? Is it in every event that happens, even in our yesterday? Is this joy in the natural part of our tomorrow?

It is imperative that we examine our thinking, and to answer these questions, rather than just accept what we were told. For most of us, when we choose to question what we have been told this will bring forth how we process the event or situation. Do we see the event with only our physical eyes, or do we see it with our spiritual sight, as well? We must recognize that we see many things without the use of our physical sight. So, if we can only see with our physical eyes, we might not understand what it was we saw, and this will create more confusion for us.

This will make us question if the experience was delusional, or did it really happen. When that happens, we find ourselves experiencing what we wanted to happen——rather than what really did happen.

Our desires become the motivation for our actions and responses. Rather than allowing ourselves the opportunity to receive that experience for what it has to bring. To recognize that there is "nothing to fear about the experience but fear itself." Take, for example, the topic of love. We all want love, but we walk into a relationship with a list or agenda of what we want it to be. Even when we get the things we want, often we tell ourselves things are not okay. Most often the nature of any plan is to project into tomorrow, and it is always uncertain. This leaves room for us to become afraid to love, because with an agenda there will always be uncertainties.

However, when we talk about true love, we are talking about a level of uncertainty, but for us to have it we must be willing to surrender to this uncertainty. That is the moment of the "now," where the joy and blessings are derived from, and we need to surrender to, to experience true love. Rather than expecting the joy or love to just come our way, because it is what we want it to be. It is imperative that we recognize that love needs our <u>participation</u> to exist. Without our full presence, love will never be there. Only the <u>idea</u> of love (or the definition of it) will show up. We have to be willing to ask the questions of ourselves, which of the two thought-systems are we using to think with? The thought-systems of "<u>fear</u> and <u>confusion</u>," or the one of "<u>love</u> and <u>peace</u>." These are critical questions for us to ask in a new way thinking.

If we have chosen the thought-system that teaches us about love and peace it will reflect the ideas of wholeness and our inner connection. All thoughts start as an idea. If we accept this as the truth, which I believe it most sincerely is, then the whole must reflect the same or one (on some connected level). This gives us a common foundation to see ourselves and others as one. So, when we allow love to give us our direction we will have no need to be afraid or a need for an agenda. We will merely be waiting for love's presence with open arms. This will become our new way of thinking.

We must be willing to surrender to a level of <u>faith,</u> which most of us struggle with, to allow a new way of thinking to come about. This will require us to let go of our old conditioning, and to make way for change. To do this we must be willing to get out of our way, and to give into the Godly voice that speaks to us every day. This voice that is telling us about the one direction of love. This requires some faith to accept that the <u>truth</u> is always right in front of us. We only need to accept this, and to hear the Godly-Voice within. This voice moves in but <u>one</u> <u>direction</u>, and that direction is toward <u>truth</u> and <u>love</u>. To accept is not about our conditions or the maybe's of our tomorrow.

Faith requires that we recognize that true love is not about "sometime," this is but a partial-view of love, and will come and go like the wind. This could <u>not</u> be the true love that God (our creator) offers us. The truth that can be altered, could <u>never</u> reflect the whole. Its level of consistency could not be maintained if we make alteration. These are the natural laws at work here making things whole, and maintaining their level of consistency, which is a reflection of truth. This would leave no room for inconsistences or changes, because the reflection of truth is always, always, always, right in front of us.

The love that God gave us is <u>changeless</u>, which explains why the truth is always in front of us. To hide it would mean to be deceitful, and there is no love in that! God shares love with all of us, and this <u>love</u> is universal and is reflected in all of God's creations. This is a new way of thinking.

Healing The Confusion

This is about recognizing the thought-system we use every day. Like I mentioned before, there are only two major thought-systems, one of <u>Love</u> and one of <u>fear</u>. These systems tells us "what is the right way or wrong way of doing things." It is also a method we used to release anxiety and fear, which the ego brings to our door regularly.

We must realize that our confusion comes to us due to our lack of understanding as to who we believe we are. If we believe that all that we are is our physical bodies, then we must be confused. Science cannot give us a clear answer to this question, of who we are, other than we are our bodies. But the body comes with vast number of limitations, and continues to decay and die. This just creates more fear and confusion about the process of death——and what happens next.

God has given us a way out of this confusion! Which allows us to use our minds, and to understand that there are no limits——to our minds. It is one complete unit, unlike the body that has many different parts. The body has a heart, brain, lymph system, circulatory system and a nervous system just to name a few of our parts. But we need to remember that the body <u>cannot</u> join, and because of that they will <u>not</u> feel the union or the holy connection of our minds. This is where healing takes place in our minds. But we must make the connection for the healing to take place.

How could God (our creator) create the body that is <u>unlike</u> itself? Our bodies have always been presented with sickness, fear, hatred, and confusion. None of these actions reflect our true strength or the clarity of our Godliness. Yet when we look at ourselves, we cannot see or recognize our spirit or that Godly place within us. Our eyes only show us the physical body, which is but a fragment of who we really are.

The diversities of bodies we see around the world confuses us on a physical level, and this tells us <u>not</u> to trust our brothers. This puts us in a state of confusion by having us believe we are <u>just</u> our bodies. We must hold on to the thought that only our minds can join; this will help us understand how we are all connected. And where healing takes place. Only when we can surrender to that holy instant, can we make our holy connection and receive the healing.

We are here merely to be receivers of reality, <u>not</u> the creator of it. Here lies the bulk of our confusion, when we think that we are in control of our reality. This is what keeps us on the roller coaster ride of life, and with such internal conflict about who we believe we are! We must be willing to change our way of thinking about our mind, in order to find peace. By accepting our spiritual path to our internal Faith we can start to erase some of our confusion. Then we will recognize that we are complete and whole, and can function without conflict.

Accepting Of Our Reality

Let us look at the reality of asking a good friend for a loan of one hundred dollars, and he told you how much he would like to loan you the money, but he only had twenty dollars. This means that it would be impossible for him to give away what he does not have. The truth of reality is that what is real is always right in front of us. Just like your friend if he does not have the money, he cannot give it to you. It is also important that we understand this, to give away a miracle of our love, we must feel it within ourselves first. This is the simplicity of reality!

> ### *"God's natural law of love states; that love needs our presence to exist."*

This means that if you are not present, neither will love be, regardless of what we tell ourselves. In wanting the healing of our minds we must learn how to see the whole. We must be willing to change our mind and recognize that only minds can communicate. But the ego will have us see things quite differently. It would have us believe that the body is complete, and that we are in total control. Our ego wants us to believe that the body can both communicate and share and yet the body in its own accord has no function without the mind.

Jill Bolte Taylor tells us in her book, My Strike of Insight, that in order to communicate with one another, we must share a certain amount of common reality. As a result, our nervous system must be virtually identical in their ability to perceive information from the external world. This helps us to process and integrate this information in our brains, and then have similar systems of output (including thoughts, words and deeds) to reflect our results.

This gives us a strong clue as to how much we are alike. The ego will often have us believe that we are self-sufficient and need no help. This approach will not strengthen us, it only serve the goal of our ego which is usually to divide or separate us.

When trying to assess truth or reality we must have a clear understanding of what it is we saw. This understanding allows us to have an appreciation and a clarity of those things we have come to identify with. This simplified method of talking about reality demonstrates that clarity is presented only by those things, we can identify with. However, this often allows us to believe in illusions, and to make them real. As I have said before those things we believe in, we will accept, because we can identify with them. Thus we will make those things our reality.

To have a clear understanding of our reality requires us to have a level of faith.

Faith is not something we can learn or be taught from a book; it is given to us by God (our creator) as our birth-right! So, it only needs to be remembered and practiced to be revealed! Through our faith we develop a true understanding of who we really are.

This will move us beyond all that we have been taught about our bodies. We begin to develop a new perception, and not just about our physical body. We are given the clarity to see what is necessary to have us recognize that we are whole. It is most important that we ask some of these questions, if I am <u>not</u> my body what am I? Who am I? Why wouldn't the spirit of my brother <u>not</u> be the same as my spirit? These are critical questions for our mental healing and for the acceptance of our true realty.

Many scholars have meditated and contemplated on this subject of <u>reality</u> for years, and yet, we continue to be confused over the subject of reality. It is hard for us to believe that all we need to do is to <u>accept</u> the event that is in front of us, without judgment. Then the clarity of our understanding will reveal true reality to us. Judgment can be a tricky topic, because it means to make a choice. These choices and judgments have always been a part of our daily lives thus making us feel as though we are in control with what is going to happen next. But if we are really honest with ourselves, we realize that we are not very accurate in recognizing what will happen next. This usually creates more internal confusion, and often a false reality. Our judgments (in most cases) are often presented as some form of attack, whether that attack is against ourselves or our brothers. We usually can never find peace when we use any form of an attack!

When we can accept our brothers and sisters as an extension of ourselves, we will start to understand our oneness and our true reality. It is in this holy instant that we can recognize our spiritual connection. Then we can begin to comprehend that nothing is required of us, just our acceptance without judgment. We try so hard to make reality our own creation, but we have forgotten the only thing required is to recognize what is in front of us, because this is where true reality is. When we have the understanding of this recognition our part becomes quite simple; we only need the courage to not alter what it is we see. However, in most cases this is always the most challenging part, brought forth by our conditioning.

We know that if we can share our love, and stay vigilant to that direction, God's natural laws will do the rest. If we can accept our natural abilities to love, regardless of how much love is applied to this _one_ directional approach, we know we will find our way to love. If we apply this same focus and ability to loving ourselves and others, what a wonderful world this would be.

How could we not be successful when using such an approach? This will allow us to begin to emphasize love, rather than focusing on our attention on separation and differences. When we can share and recognize our sameness, we will begin to heal the wounds of our division thus allowing us to see reality differently. As we heal, so will our brothers heal. This allows us to recognize that we are never alone. Only in our separateness, can we be alone. And this can only be a false reality.

Poor Perception

Our poor perceptions often creates problems for us, because it has us focusing only on what our eyes present to us. This is when we thought we saw one thing and later realized that it was totally different. And telling ourselves what the outcome should be, because it is what we want it to be. These are but poor perceptions created by our egos keeping us confused. Without having a clear understanding of how to perceive things with a right-minded understanding, we will often perceive poorly. Our ego's method of perception is derived out of fear and confusion.

Accurate perception deals with clarity and a universal understanding given to us by God (our creator). This universal gift has no need of conflict or chaos. Clear perception awaken us to our right-mindedness, allowing us to realize that <u>love</u> is what we are here to learn, and to share. Love is, and has always been without fear or conflict. So, when we are not truthful to ourselves, we find that we become troubled and fearful over any situation or circumstance we find ourselves in. This is where our thoughts create our projections and poor perception of fear, and these thoughts will not bring forth any level of reality or peace of mind.

Poor perception will usually lead us to a place in our thoughts that brings on deception and confusion making reality what we want it to be, rather than accepting what it is. There can never be real peace in the dreams of tomorrow, because true reality can only be found in the acceptance of the now.

Kenneth J Gergen book, <u>The Saturated Self</u>, expresses the modernist view that the world is made up of various essences or "natural Kinds" — physical atoms, chemical elements, psychological states, and social institutions. These various fields of endeavor—physics, chemistry, psychology, are there to inform the culture about the nature of a particular class of entities. This led to an increasing awareness of multiplicity, and a perspective (meaning the things around them) that often distorted their point of view.

However, this perspective is generally dependent on situations carried from our past, which usually are biased by our own old values and ideology we have placed on them, and bonded by the constraint of literary convention. If we continue to entertain this ambiguous related approach of ourselves, how could we <u>not</u> be conflicted, and with poor perception?

This would only lead us to not see the value in our brothers. This is more about us just rejecting the physical body that is appearing before us. We are not able to recognize their <u>spirit,</u> which is a continuous part of us that we usually do not recognize. This will usually have us feeling lost and alone, because we do <u>not</u> recognize our gifts. It means we must have forgotten how to embrace our differences, and this will create a split-mind. Freud describes this as our altered self ("our ego"). It is that part of us that wants to be divided and separate. Being in this state of mind will not allow us to embrace our diversity.

So, the ego will win, and direct our thoughts to the idea of Me, Mine, or I, thought-system. With this thought-system, we want to be right and have a strong need to be in control. This self-gratifying system continues to show us our differences, and this will always create a line between us and others. We have felt and been taught that those things that are different cannot be trusted. We have learned this through our conditioning. What we have forgotten is the appearance of a person does not change his spiritual value, and that we are all one in spirit. We need only to look inside to recognize the truth of our oneness. The differences we see are there for our growth, and through our diversity we can understand that spiritual love reflects no difference. This allows us to see with a clearer perception.

It is important for us to look inward for our answers to the questions of peace and love. Once we have found this peace and love we will no longer feel <u>lost</u> or <u>alone</u>, because we will then recognize our love of self is what we must be willing to share with others. Love by its nature has but <u>one</u> direction and moves without fear. We only need to embrace this direction of love. Then poor perception will disappear, like the darkness when we add light.

Awaking To Our Right Mindedness

By awaking to this right mindedness it is important we recognize that it is love that really counts. However, our poor perception allows us to deny that we are the source of our power and our love. This perception is the driving force of our confusion, and to the loss of our power to our egos. This will then become the creator of our split-mindedness, and until we recognize this, we will continue to believe that we are lost and alone.

The ego is quite clever in the ways of deception. It will often show us division, rather than union, as a method of deception. It does not want us to see what we share with anyone else. It continues to tell us stories about the people we see daily, and have us register them as just other bodies. By telling us there is nothing special about them, we don't make a meaningful connection. Here again is the deception of our egos creating a split-mind and creating more confusion.

When we do not feel our connection, we will <u>not</u> feel our union. Then fear will become the means of our separation, and this is the energy of our ego. Truth is the reflection of clarity, and much like love, it creates no deceptions. It is a very impractical thought for us to believe that we can make truth be what we want it to be. Neither <u>Truth</u> nor <u>Love</u> can be defined or called upon at will to make it be what we want or think it should be. This is the thought process of fantasies and illusions, and is driven by the confusion of our poor perception, which holds us captive to our illusions. It make us believe that reality can be what we would like it to be. So, if we try to change what is in front of us to something else, can we call it reality? When will it stop?

Considering that we do have the power of choice, and recognizing there are only two outcomes to our choices: either we are looking for the truth or we are looking at illusions and lies. They are opposite by nature, and can not be on the same side of the coin. We cannot have or know love, and be fearful of it, because if we do, perhaps what we have is <u>not</u> love. Love by its nature cannot be partial and be whole at the same time. This, again, becomes one of our painted illusions: to see a small part and label it to be the whole. Often this is one of the hardest things to change about our perceptions; to allow ourselves the opportunity to change our minds, about what we believe. We are far more than just our body that image of us reflected back from the mirror. We need to let ourselves see beyond our body, so we may recognize our union, and awaken to our spiritual self.

Think about all the times that our wife or husband, lover, friend, or even our parents have told us how much *they love us*—and we believed them. However, over time their actions never proved to be that kind of the love we wanted to feel in our heart. Their love did not come with any level of understanding. This can become quite confusing, because we made the choice to frame our own life this way, and over time have chosen to accept it as love. I think of love like awaking to our right-mindedness, which reveals the obvious with clarity and understanding.

Society has helped paint this picture for us by its continued deception of love. Telling us of partial truths and echoing it through our parents or teachers to represent the truth. So, what are we to believe when the people that we love and trust tells us, about the things that we believe are true? This is why we will find it to be one of the hardest lessons we will ever have to learn. To allow ourselves a chance to change our minds about what it is we created. We must allow ourselves a chance to experience reality, rather than believing we created it. Much like love, it is there to be experienced— not created. To recognize this will allow us to no longer feel lost, or afraid, because we will have acquired clarity. With this new mode of thinking it will help us recognize that we are never alone. We will then see there is always strength in numbers, and to recognize the idea of "*we*" and see that <u>we</u> is always about sharing and union—not separation.

Have you ever had a friend who is on the other side of the world, but calls you to tell you how much he misses you, or to pass along his condolences of a lost loved one? We can sometimes feel the connection even though we are separated by thousands of miles. This is how right-mindedness opens us to our union and oneness. This allows us to feel the love of our oneness and the connection that transcend time and space.

How is this possible? Can it be about something greater than our physical bodies? It can become so real sometimes that we can almost feel their presence. This again talks about the <u>limitlessness</u> of love itself, which cannot be defined by a word, because there are no words that could express its true meaning. This is why we find it so hard to tell someone what we are feeling, because a feeling is a sensation to be experienced by oneself and then shared with others. And this always require our participation for any experience to be shared.

The human nervous system is a wonderfully dynamic entity, composed of an estimated one trillion cells. To give us some appreciation for how enormous one trillion is, consider that there are approximately six-billion people on the planet, and it is said that we would have to multiply all six-billion people times 166 times just to make up the number of cells to create a single nervous system.

Jill Bolte Taylor, in her book <u>My Stroke of Insight,</u> tells us that as members of the same human species, we share all but 0.01 percent (1/100 of 1 percent) of identical genetic sequences. So, biologically speaking, as a species, we are virtually identical to one another at the level of our genes (99.99 percent).

So, when we look around us at the diversity within the human race, it is obvious that this 0.01 percent accounts for a significant difference in how we look. However, with all the evidence provided to our sameness, we continue to see ourselves quite differently at a spiritual level. Perhaps, this is because we do <u>not</u> recognize our own spiritual self— as of yet.

What Does It Mean To Be Conditioned?

Does it mean that we have lost our freedom? Can we say that there is anyone we know who has not been conditioned on some level? In talking about conditioning I think it would be fair to say that we have all been conditioned. We have been taught to be reactionary to images we see, because usually there was no clarity brought to the images. Most of our conditioning was brought on by our parents, and by society in general.

Actually we never gave much thought to the actions of our parents as a form of conditioning. However, as we have gotten older we realize that our parents did <u>not</u> have all the right answers. But that was okay, because now we are capable of making our own decisions. Unfortunately for most of us, we have failed to look at or take note of our conditioning. Not only did our parents not tell us how to approach this part of our lives, but society and our culture reinforced it as well. We were told what to do and when to do it. However, this message was not about love or clarity, but about the rules of society, and its direction.

For most of us, this is just the way things were done, because it was the way we were taught. Classical conditioning was introduced by a Russian scientist named Ivan Pavlov, who was trained in biology and medicine (much like his contemporary Sigmund Freud). Pavlov was studying the digestive track of animals, when he started to observe the response by the dogs who salivated when his assistant came in with food. The response of salivation became quite intriguing to him, and caused him to change his direction of study. His investigation revealed an interesting phenomenon, and from this he established the laws of Classical

Conditioning. Classical conditioning starts with a reflex: an innates; involuntary behavior. It elicits a response that you are <u>not</u> in control of, and yet, you are very much a part of. For example, when we go to the optometrist and he blows the air into our eye, and we blink from the air it is an involuntary reaction. Or when our heart flutters, from an escape of a near accident, realizing it was a close call. In classical conditioning there is no new behavior learned. So, instead, we developed an association which is developed through pairing between the <u>natural stimulus</u> (NS) (which does not elicit a response) and the *unconditioned stimulus* (US) (which elicits a response) so that all of us can experience both responses.

Knowing

The idea of knowing has always been there for us to understand. However, the ego does not want us to <u>know</u> or to look for the truth. It realizes that this would undermine the power we have given to our egos. The ego wants us to dwell in our past, and to look for sound data that makes it reliable, so we may tell ourselves we have the correct answers.

Societies and cultures have done this for centuries (telling us what we should know), so who are <u>we</u> to make changes to the way things are done? By choosing to hold on to our understanding of yesterday, we have also chosen to stay trapped by that informational source. Which is often steaming from our past, and we are now trying to make it real. This source does _not_ reveal truth or knowing; it only reflects what we have learned, and have chosen to make real.

Usually the information from our past can only reveal partial information. Which only create answers that allows us to feel good about the direction we have chosen. But this does not reveal truth. When we learn to surrender to the right direction it will always be right in front of us. However, this can only happen if we are willing to see what is there, and _not_ what we _want_ to be there. Our desires do not create truth or the right direction for us. This can only be revealed to us, by our willingness to recognize that we are Godly. Truth has but _one_ direction and this is how _knowing_ is revealed to us. The realization of what is in front of us, is not about the past (nor the future), it only about the now which is all that's real.

To know is not about _form,_ but is about _content_. We can only have knowing if we are willing to search ourselves for our own discovery. Recognizing that each event which is right in front of us, is there for our growth and guidance, to help us understand what it is we don't know.

Knowing comes with the blessing of faith, that requires an invitation from us to be revealed. Without the understanding of our blessings we will not be able to see or recognize the _content_ of the experience, we will only see the form. Peace delivers the means for us to understand which is always about content. So, we must recognize that we need both peace and understanding for us to have knowing. It is important for us to realize that we can only acquire peace if we are willing to give up the thought-system of attacks or fear. This thought-system is always driven by confusion and fear. This means we must be willing to let go of the thought-system of our ego, so we may see the greater part of ourselves.

Science has told us that we are more alike than not, and yet, we continue to focus on that tiny part of us (our body) that bring on our fears and our differences. Remember, the ego needs for us to believe that we are different, and it shows us this by the many *things* our eyes deliver us.

Yes! There are many thing that are different between us, but this does not have to create separation for us. So, when we make the choice to accept our differences, we are accepting that tiny part (our diversity), and giving it more value than our union. We must understand that if we choose the thought-system of our egos, it is based on control and separation—thus supporting the idea of our confusion and fears.

The understanding of peace comes with its own miracles, which is happening around us all the time. But often we are too busy to recognize them. We cannot have peace without understanding, because they come as a total package—and so do we! Then we will start to hear the voice of love that is always there guiding our path to the direction of peace!

Most of the objects that appear before us do not always represent love. They are just things or objects which have no real value of their own accord. We often choose to give them value or power to make them valuable to us, thus giving <u>form</u> value over <u>content</u>. When we choose to create this kind of value, we usually use attacks (rather than love) as our mode of action. This could never be a process of <u>knowing</u>, because it comes with no peace or understanding as part of it foundation.

Clarity Of Thought

To question will often manifest as fear inside of us (and not love) due to our lack of understanding. Most of us see what is in front of us, but we do not see the <u>content</u> of what is there. We only see its form. We find ourselves trapped by this <u>form</u> or the messages passed on by our identification with the form. And often, in many cases the objects may <u>not</u> be what they appear to be, at all. We need to allow ourselves to look closer, so we may see the content of what is being revealed. Then this will allow us to process the event, and receive the blessings and guidance of that moment, and it's content. This is what brings on <u>clarity of thought</u> and peace of mind that accompanies it.

This requires very little effort on our part, but it does ask for us to surrender, so we may recognize what is there— right in front of us. This will only appear to be difficult when we have a conflicted or confused mind. Because with a conflicted mind, we cannot have any level of clarity or understanding of our inner-being.

This would imply that we believe our ego has the power and the means to be victorious. To have this kind of internal conflict (or war) we must have acknowledged it presence, and have a willingness to use the approach of fear and confusion— over love. We need to recognize that any conflict must be a process that occurs between two forces, and must be made out of choice.

The book, A Course in Miracles states that "Truth does not fight against illusions, nor does an illusion fight against the truth." Illusions only battle against illusions. It is important that we understand this to recognize the choices we make. When we seek any answers outside of ourselves we have chosen to accept the illusion as real, thus allowing ourselves to create a false truth or a false reality.

This then will become our foundational wisdom of our egos: seek and you shall not find. This approach will never yield any clarity of thought. The ego cannot share clarity or love with any of us; it can only tell us about it, in definitions. It is critically important that we recognize that love can only reflect itself. If this is so, it would have no contrast or definition! However, the ego will eagerly tell us, what it should be, thus giving it an opposite to what it is.

Clarity of thought can only come from the oneness that we chose to share with ourselves and others. If we are not able to recognize this clarity in ourselves, we will find it hard to see it in our brothers and sisters of the world. The ego is not aware of this clarity or love. It only functions through definitions, which it has pieced together from our thoughts. True understanding can only come from one's inner-self, which speaks with us every day. This is our spiritual-connection that allows us to recognize that we are all one in spirit.

The ego would have us see the body of our brothers or sisters, and only focus on our differences. Thus giving us a reason to see and focus on the many things we share that are different, and yet, this is such a small part of us. We must go inside and search for our spiritual connection so we may express the greater part of us. Which is what brings forth our clarity.

We talk about being religious (and wanting to love our fellow man), but that seems to be just talk— if we do <u>not</u> see our likeness. This likeness cannot be just a reflection of our physical self, be-cause the ego has already shown us that we are different physically. So, we must learn to see with the sight of our inner-vision (spirit) to reflect our likeness and clarity.

Looking At Our Mind

I have often spoken of us, as being "Godly" because (regardless of what we have been told), that is exactly what we are— "Godly." We only need to get beyond the idea that we are just our bodies! The mind is what allows us to be connected. How often have we called upon our partner or spouse to do something, when they were miles away from us? And yet, the job or task was done. Like when we have told our partner to bring something home from the market—without ever speaking a word to them personally. Has this ever happen to you? Or, to send some love to the other side of the world, and your partner or friend receives it and this is verified by them calling the next day.

This is what is meant by "spiritual-connection." It is not just from our thoughts that we make this connection, but it is from our minds that we realize our source. This becomes an example of our inner-voice that speaks to us every day, and yet, is so often denied. This is the voice that tells us to love, because love is the only way to go that makes any sense. And yet we make love a condition! When we make love a condition we give it options or contrasts. Which means it would have to be built on specific criterion. This will give it the ability to have multiple outcomes, which will never make us happy. Because we have a problem in defining what happiness means for ourselves. These outcomes are based on our own projections, which create illusions or false reality. Our desires do not make reality real or meaningful, it only makes it confusing. Here again is the thought-system we choose to use to make our choices. The one that tells us to seek—but do not find!

When we think of our minds we often think of our brains at that same moment. But our brain and the mind are two different systems in the body. Our fore fathers have been saying this for thousands of years. Plato, Socrates, Aristotle, spoke of this when they talked about "the spirit," as it relates to the mind.

The mind was given to us so that the Godliness within us could never be silenced.

The mind was given to recognize the light within us, which will always shine and can never be extinguished! This part of us is eternal, and is connected to our "Godly self."

We must be willing to be connected with our spiritual-self in order to recognize this light. Only then can we recognize this light in our brothers, because we must first acknowledge this light in ourselves. This acknowledgment allows us to feel the "connection," and to know that we are not "alone." The ego wants to keep us in state of confusion about the direction of our lives, and about the decisions we make every day. It wants us to believe that <u>we</u> are in control, and that the chaos can be reconciled. But if we think about it for just a second or two, we will realize that we are just participants in the process of reality—not the creator of it!

The primary goal of the ego is to have us see <u>form</u> over <u>content</u>. We are led to believe that whatever we have created has great value and should be cherished. However, <u>form</u> can not reflect the truth, it can only project an image! The ego does not have the ability to see or recognize clarity, but this is a major part of understanding <u>content</u>. It needs to keep us confused about what we see and what we should value. For example, we have told ourselves that we need a new dress for our upcoming party on Friday night, but we also realized we had no money. Yet, we talk ourselves into buying a new dress for the party. Then we fight with ourselves over that decision. We have made our value predicated on what others will think if we show up in an old dress. Even though they have never seen the dress we are now wearing. This is where we have allowed <u>form</u> to keep us confused. We must understand that the ego is very clever in helping us to see the value in the things we have created. But it just clouds our mind to what is real.

The ego allows us to believe that we are in control of today and our tomorrows. But it never tells us that this is impossible, because tomorrow can never be under our control. It does this by allowing us to have these projections or fantasies, and telling us what "should happen" in our tomorrow. But here again, it is telling us about <u>form</u>, and not about <u>content</u>. It is based on the idea of tomorrow, and tomorrow is not here yet— and cannot be real. It can only be our perception of the reality that we want it to be.

It is important that we understand that reality is dynamic by its nature and can never be in our control. It comes from form which is always changing and will never be the same —only similar. Where is the clarity and understanding in that which is always changing? The ego tells us if we see it with our own eyes, then it must be real. Yes, the object, in most cases, is quite real (in our physical realm), but it often lacks clarity and consistence.

So, without the clarity and consistence, how could we understand its content? Content has to come with substance for it to be understood. It is like "our union" (which gives us a sense of oneness) which allows for the truth to be discovered. The truth cannot be discovered alone. It requires our union and love. As I mentioned earlier, that love needs our presence to exist. Without our presence, love is but a thought in our head—never to be shared or realized.

It is the sharing of love that makes love what it is, and we need "union" for this sharing to take place. Sharing starts with our <u>intent of heart</u>, which allows us to recognize that we are one in spirit and in our minds. And can never be alone!

CHAPTER 3
The Social Influence

T here are many things around us that direct our lives. The list would cover a number of topics from sports, music, art, medicine and science and a long list of sub-topics like (1) Social influence, which can take on many forms and can be seen as conformity, peer pressure, or obedience (2) The concept of social influence is defined by the changes made in our individual thoughts, feelings, attitude or behaviors, as they affect others. These conformities may also be seen as persuasion, sales, marketing and technology (i.e. cell phone). Conformity occurs when an individual expresses a particular opinion or behavior in order to fit into a given situation, and to meet the expectations of a given order. Conformity does not necessarily hold an opinion or belief that the behavior is appropriate, as stated by Herbert Kelman. In 1958, Harvard psychologist Herbert Kelman identified that there are three broad varieties of social influence.

- <u>Compliance</u> is when people appear to agree with others, but actually keep their dissenting opinion private.
- <u>Identification</u> is when people are influenced by someone who is liked and respected, such as a famous celebrity.
- <u>Internalization</u> is when people accept a belief or behavior and agree both publicly and privately.

Morton Deutsch and Harold Gerard described two psychological needs that humans must have to conform to the expectation of others. These include our need to be right in an informational social influence and our need to be liked (normative social influence). <u>Informational</u> <u>influence</u> (or social proof) is a form of influence to accept information from another as evidence about reality. Informational influence comes into play when people are uncertain, either because of stimuli are intrinsically ambiguous, or because there is social disagreement. <u>Normative</u> <u>influence</u> is an influence to conform to the positive expectation of others. In terms of Kilman's typology, normative influence leads to public compliance, whereas informational influence leads to private acceptance.

There are three processes of attitude changes that are defined by Harvard psychologist Herbert Kelman in his 1958 paper in the "Journal of Conflict Resolution." He thought, defining these processes would help determine the effects of social influence. For example, to separate public conformity (behavior) from private acceptance (personal belief). The question arises: do I comply out of coercion, or do I comply out of belief? *Compliance* is the act of responding favorably to an explicit or implicit request offered by others. The reality is that compliance is a change in behavior but not necessarily in one's attitude. One can comply due to mere obedience, or by otherwise holding back his private thoughts, due to social pressures.

According to Kelman's 1958 paper, the satisfaction derived from compliance is due to the social effect of the accepting influence (i. e, people comply for a reward or out of fear of punishment). When we have i*dentification* there is a change in attitude and behavior due to the influence of someone famous or who is well-liked.

Advertisements and media use celebrity's identifications to market their products and sell their company's merchandise. *Internalization* is the process of accepting a set of rules or norm established by people or groups who are influential to other individuals. In this case, the individuals accept the influence because the content of the influence is intrinsically accepted as rewarding. It is congruent with the individual's value system. They believe in the thought system which they have been taught (and made to believe in), and that is why they would want to be a part of that group.

When we are born, we do not have a set of values and expectations, so we learn them from our parents or other adults who raise us as our primary caregivers. We learn not only through these adults who teach us, but also by our experiences, and by watching and observing others.

As we grow up and get to an age when we start to understand what "values" are, we then can begin to internalize our own values. This allows us to have an understanding of what is right or wrong about our actions, and what they really mean. Our values and expectations are subjective principles; and we will sometimes do wrong just to see what it feels like. Since we have never been given a clear understanding of right or wrong, only guidelines were given to us, either by society or our parents. Since we spend most of our time with our families, they would be the primary adults who influence and give value to our expectations. We were never taught to look at nurture as opposed to nature, for our sound understanding. This debate has gone on for a long time, and has continued to raise questions by researchers as to which approach is best. Is it our environment or family that shapes and molds our behavior? Or, is it our genes and genetic make-up that determines the way we act? It is almost impossible to be certain as to the exact amount the environment has influenced us. If you think about it, everyone has a different interaction with the environment. We talk about how the family influences our values, but it also depends on how much time, we spend with our family. If our parents are only home for short periods of time, then the family would have less of an impact on the child, in comparison to the stay-at-home parent.

Looking At The Family Value System

This will also depends on the value system of the parents who are rearing the child. What are the parent's values? Are they based on authoritative values, or a more liberal value system? Let us look at a family that spends at least 80 to 85% of the hour awake with their children. The influences and values would be quite significant, because of the amount of time given to their interaction with each other.

Take another example of animals in general. When they are born, they stay close to their kin so they may learn how to hunt and survive, and gradually they learn to survive on their own. Humans are much the same way, we are strongly influenced by our observations. We are heavily influences by our parents, or the primary care givers with whom we spent those early years.

On the other hand, if that child spends more time with others their values and expectations will be influenced by outside sources. We were quite impressionable in our youth. For example, if our parents are religious, we might choose that direction. If our parents are drinkers, smokers, or drug user this can become a habit we pick up, as well. We cannot choose our parents or alter the influences they put upon us, so it is up to us to discover our own value system about what is right. We must ask ourselves what is right, and what Truth is for us—— allowing us to create our own value system. It is important that we ask ourselves, who are we really? We need to learn how to not depend on the influences of our parents. We need to realize they were conditioned by the same thought-system which produced our confusion and compliance.

Conformity

Conformity is a type of social influence that is involved with change in both belief and behavior. We make these changes in order to fit in with a particular group. It is the most common and the most pervasive form of social influence. The term conformity is often used to indicate an agreement to join the majority position. There have been many experiments in social psychology investigations on conformity. The first to study it was Jenness in 1932. His experiment was an ambiguous situation involving a glass bottle filled with beans. He ask participants individually to estimate how many beans the bottle contained. Later he used a group approach through discussion to estimate the number. Participants were again asked to estimate the number to find whether their initial estimate had changed based on the influence of the majority. Jenness' finding was that almost all of the participants choose to change their initial estimate implying the effect of the majority rule.

The types of social conformity: Compliance or Normative, informational and internalization. Kelman (1958) distinguished the three types of conformity: yielding to the pressure because a person wants to fit in with the group, or conforming due to fear of being rejected by that group. Which often leads us to public or group compliance, but not necessarily private acceptance of that group's social norms.

Informational conformity usually occurs when a person lacks knowledge and looks to the group for guidance. Or when a person is in an ambiguous or unclear situation and socially compares their behavior with the group.

This type of conformity usually involves <u>internalization</u> (also called social proof), or internalization in Kelman's terms. Which means publicly we are willing to change our position to fit with the group and also agreeing with them privately.

Non Conformity

Not everyone conforms to social pressure. Indeed, there are many factors that contribute to an individual's desire to remain independent of the group. For example, Smith and Bond (1998) discovered cultural differences in conformity between western and eastern countries. People from western cultures (such as America and the UK) are more likely to be individualistic and don't want to be seen as being the same as everyone else. This mean they value being independent and self-sufficient (the individual is more important than the group), and as such are more likely to participate in non-conformity.

In contrast, eastern cultures (such as Asian countries) are more likely to value the need of the family and other social groups before their own.

Media exerts normative social influence by publicizing deviation from the norms of a particular group or society. This influence will result in a different point of view of the norm. Media influences are used in media studies, psychology, communication theory and sinology, to refer to the theories about the ways in which mass media affects how their audiences think and behave. These studies brought on concerns in the early mid-20th century as to whether the media has weakened or limited the individual's capacity to act autonomously.

Often, a large amount of control is placed on the content which society watches. This control or content of the news media has the ability to alter the participation and habits of the public. The internet has also opened the door to more political opinions, and to social and cultural viewpoints with a higher level of participation. Theorists such as Louis Wirth and Talcott Parsons have emphasized the importance of mass media as an instrument of social control. They state that the rise of the internet, (and the two-way relationship between mass media and public opinion) is beginning to change with the advent of new technologies (such as blogging).

Technology

What is technology but a continuation of evolution by other means: When *a* scientist states that something is possible he is almost certainly right. When he states that something is impossible, he is very likely to be wrong. This was proposed by Arthur C. Clarke in the essay "Hazards of prophecy: The Failure of Imagination" in Profiles of the Future 1962.

The word "technology" is derived from the Greek tekhnos, which means "craft or art," and logia, which means "the study of." Thus, one interpretation of technology is the study of crafting, in which crafting refers to the shaping of resources, for a particular purpose. I use the term resources rather than materials, because technology extends to the shaping of nonmaterial resources (such as information) and this is indeed possible.

Technology is often defined as the creation of tools to gain control over the environment. The uniqueness of us as humans is that we have acquired the knowledge and the ability to record and reuse the information acquired. This knowledge represents our ability to process the evolving technology. As our technology has evolved, so has the means for recording this data. It starts from the oral tradition of antiquity to the written design and logs of nineteenth century craftsmen and the computer assisted design databases of the 1990s.

Technology also implies a transcendence of the materials used to comprise it. What I mean by this is, when the elements of an invention are assembled in just the right way, they can produce an enchanting <u>effect</u> that goes beyond the mere parts. We are not always certain of how these parts are to fit together. But when materials are used with modern technology, the outcome of the assembly can be transcendent (i.e. computers). The assembled object becomes greater than the sum of its parts. The same phenomenon of transcendence occurs in art, which can be regarded as another form of human technology. When wood is carved and varnished, and strings are assembled in just the proper way, the result is wondrous (violins or guitars are created). When these instruments are manipulated in just the right way, a miracle of another sort takes place and music is born. As a musician, I've learned that music goes beyond just the sound. It evokes a response of cognitive emotion, and perhaps in some cases a spiritual connection in the listener.

Language And Technology

Our language is another form of human-created technology in a different kind of way. One of the primary applications of this technology is communication. Communication is a critical survival skill in the times we live. It provides for families and tribes to develop cooperative strategies to overcome obstacles and adversaries. All animals communicate. Monkeys and apes use elaborate gestures and grunts to communicate a variety of messages. Bees perform intricate dances in a figure-eight pattern to communicate where the next batch of nectar can be found. Crabs wave their claws in one way to alert others of the danger of adversaries, but used in a different way for courtship. However, these methods of communication do not appear to evolve, other than through the usual DNA based evolution. These species lack a way to record their means of communication, so their method of evolution remains static from one generation to the next.

However, in contrast, the human language <u>does</u> evolve, just like all forms of technology. The evolving form of our language has provided ever-improving means for recording and distributing the human language. Once life took hold on our planet, it can be stated that the emergence of <u>technology</u> <u>was</u> <u>inevitable</u>. The ability to continue to change and to reach one's physical capabilities (not to mention mental faculties) through technology is clearly useful for our survival. Technology requires two attributes of its creator: intelligence and physical ability to manipulate its environment.

The Master Piece Of Evolution

Evolution is a natural phenomenon, thus giving it the name of master programmer. It has been prolific in the designing of millions of species with breathtaking magnificence and with diversity and ingenuity. These programs have all been written down, and recorded as digital data in the chemical structure of an ingenious molecule encoding. This genetic instruction is used in the development and functioning of all living organisms, and is called <u>deoxyribonucleic</u> <u>acid</u>, or DNA.

DNA was first described by J. D. Watson and F.H. Crick in 1953 as a double helix consisting of a twisting pair of strands of polynucleotides. DNA is made of simple units that line up in a particular order, within this large molecule. The order of these units carries genetic information (called traits), similar to how the order of these words on this page carry information. The language used by DNA is called the genetic code. This information is encoded at each ledge of a spiral staircase, encoded by the choice of nucleotides.

DNA code controls the silent details of the construction of every cell in the organism. This genetic code identifies which features are inherited, and how these features are passed on from generation to generation. In a process called translation, this is where other enzymes translate the coded DNA information by building proteins. It is these proteins that define the structure, behavior, and intelligence of each cell of the organism. This is part of our understanding of the hardware of the computational engine driving life as we know it today. We are just beginning to unravel the mysteries of our human software.

Let us first praise evolution. It has created a plethora of designs of indescribable beauty with complexity, and elegance—not to mention its profound efficiency.

Some of the thoughts of aesthetics definition of beauty has to some degree been quite emulating, by the natural beauty, which evolution has created.

The Natural Progression

Evolution has achieved an extraordinary record of design, yet has taken an extraordinary long period of time to do this. We must look at some of the factors in its achievements, by its ponderousness of change in its pace. We need to conclude that its intelligence quotient is only infinitesimally greater than zero. An IQ of only slightly greater than zero (defining truly arbitrary behavior as zero) is enough for evolution to beat entropy and create wonderful designs, if given enough time. Evolution has been a growth process, and the means to evaluate time itself, which has produced the changes we see every day.

When looking at <u>evolution</u>, we don't need to look too far to see some of the wonderful gifts of this technology, and some of the universal laws brought forth by evolution. The more we allow our clarity to shine through, the greater we can see the <u>master-piece.</u> With the evolving process of evolution this is how inventions become reality, like that of Charles Babbage, who set dreaming about a table of logarithms, wondering how he could have numbers calculated by machinery. Babbage became devoted to unprecedented visions, thus creating the world's first programmable computer.

Based entirely on the mechanical technology of the nineteenth century, Babbage's "Analytical Engine" was a remarkable leader of the modern computer. Babbage developed a liaison with Ada Lovelace, who became as obsessed with the project as Babbage.

She contributed many of the ideas for programming the machine, including the invention of the programming loop and the subroutine. She was the first software engineer, prior to the twentieth century.

By the 1940s, the British government was preparing for the invasion of the German army as Hitler was marching through Europe. So the British government assembled the best mathematical minds and electrical engineers (under the leadership of Alan Turing). Their sole purpose was to break the German military code. It was already established that the German air force had a superior position in the skies, and failure to break the code would have surely doom the nation. Turing and his colleagues constructed the world's first operational computer (from telephone relays) and named it **Robinson**. The group succeeded brilliantly, and provided the British with transcriptions of nearly all Nazi messages, even as the Germans created more complexity to their codes. Turing replaced Robinson's electromagnetic intelligence with an electronic vision called **Colossus,** built from two thousand radio tubes. Colossus and nine similar machines (running in parallel) provided an uninterrupted decoding of vital military intelligence to the Allied war effort.

In addition to having established much of the theoretical foundations of computation, and having invented the operational computer, he was instrumental in the early efforts to apply this new technology to the <u>emulation of intelligence</u>. This was the birth of <u>artificial intelligence</u>. In his classic paper of 1950, ("Computing

Machinery and Intelligence"), Turing described an agenda that would impact the next half century of advances in computer research. The advancements included decision making, natural language understanding, translation, theorem proving, and (of course), encryption and the cracking of codes.

> *"We are the master-piece, and when we are able to surrender and accept this fact. We would have acknowledged our spiritual-connection, and will feel complete and whole."*

Changing Times

During the 1960s, the academic field of <u>artificial</u> <u>intelligence</u> (AI) began to complete the agenda Turing had laid out in the decade before, with encouraging or frustrating results, depending on your point of view. The 1980s saw the early signs of commercial use of <u>artificial</u> <u>intelligence,</u> with a wave of new companies forming and going public. Machines with sharply-focused intelligence became increasingly pervasive in our lives.

By the mid 1990s, the Artificial Intelligence had infiltrated the financial institutions. It had created a system that used powerful statistical and adaptive techniques. By this time the stock and bond markets (along with the currency and commodity markets) had evolved, and were now maintained by a computerized network system. With this new process, the majority of buy-and-sell decisions were initiated by these new software programs. The efficiency of this new software system created the 1987 stock market crash, and the new system was (in part) to blame. This was due to the large volume of transactions, and the rapid interaction of the new trading programs used. The old trends of processing data would have taken weeks, but now they were being processed in minutes. The use of the new algorithms allowed information and data to be processed at speeds never before achieved, which lead to the crash.

This speaks to our changing times, and the natural progression that comes with it. We need to adjust and "get out of our way" to allow the changes to be revealed. Remember, we do <u>not</u> create reality, we are merely the <u>observers</u> of that reality. Change represents changes for us, and we must be willing to embrace this process, and not become trapped by what we want it to be. We merely need to accept what is there.

Change is an evolutionary process we can <u>not</u> stop or alter. However, sometimes we believe we can, so we continue to try —— thus creating this internal conflict within ourselves. The expansion of the computer was the natural next step in the changing of times.

Computers And Their Influences

Computers have influenced us across a wide spectrum, and in so many ways that it is hard to imagine our lives without computerization. Computers are used everywhere: in schools, at home, in hospitals, banks, government institutions and on and on. One of the bad aspects of the computer is that our children use the computer for hours at a time. This has made the computer a replacement for the human connection. Children develop the skill of playing and learning on the computer (from a very early age), and a lot of parents have failed to understand the harm that it can bring.

According to some of the latest research studies on the use of computers, it has shown some serious damages to our long-term health. Children can experience many of the same related health issues brought on by the use of computers, just like adults. Extensive viewing of the computer screen can lead to eye discomfort, fatigue, blurred vision and headaches. However, some unique aspects of how children use computers may make them more susceptible than adults to developing some of these health issues.

Computer users can experience acute and chronic neck and shoulder pain. Being an acupuncturist, I see this condition far too often. Optometry doctors have seen an increase in the number of patients with eye strain, due to over use of computers. This has led to the American Optometric Association (AOA) designation of Computer Vision Syndrome. According to the AOA definition, Computer Vision Syndrome (CVS) is "the complexity of eye and vision problems related to work, which are experienced during or related to computer use." The symptoms that occur most often are eyestrain, headaches, blurred distance or near vision, along with dry or red eyes. There can also be some double vision with light sensitivity. These factors most often contribute to CVS in children, and are a combination of improper classroom conditions, play stations, or poor lighting. When we work or play at the computer for hours at a time, we need to read and analyze many things all at the same time. What happens to our eyes while we are trying to adjust to the pressure and stimuli of the screen? For this reason, we can assert that the computer really does have a negative impact on our eyesight.

Technology Of Our Times

In today's modern technology, computers have influenced our lives in ways we could have never thought possible. Computer technology is so much a part of our lives that we find it almost impossible to function without them.

They handle most of the storage, and manage enormous amounts of information we use daily. We no longer have a need to remember phone numbers of our friends or family, because they are stored in our contact list, or we get them from recent calls. Computers can operate at incredible speeds, saving us time and effort to a large extent. Computer technology can be traced back to early calculators and punch cards introduced by Allen Turing in 1936-37, which were some of the earliest computing devices.

Here is another critical question presented by Ray Kurzwell in his book <u>The</u> <u>Age</u> <u>of</u> <u>Spiritual</u> <u>Machines</u>, for the understanding of the twenty-first century: *"Can an intelligence create another intelligence more intelligent than itself?"* Let us consider this question for a moment, by looking at some of our own creations.

Evolution, (like eternity), cannot be stopped by us, or by time, as we know it. Evolution is the master programmer—— of creation. This goes beyond the idea of a machine or the data of a computer. We need to learn how to reconnect to one another and to allow our love to shine through. We must recognize that all tools are but instruments to aid us in our growth. When we lose sight of this fact, we lose sight of our <u>humanity,</u> by giving the tools <u>real</u> value. Rather than a functional value that helps us to grow.

Computers are a part of our times, and its technological design has shown us what role it places in our lives. Remember, the computer is but a <u>tool</u> to add to a better life, and not to be in control of our lives! For example, when we added speech synthesis to the program of a computer, which allow those person with speech problems to speak. This feature is just a tool that makes our life more convenient. It also allows other people, with no hands, the ability to give and receive messages, and this is beautiful process. While we have added a technical complexity to the program (and some humanlike communication skills), we still did not regard the computer to be the author of the message. Or did we?

Suppose we did not explicitly program the message in the computer, but allowed it to bring forth its own circumstances, which contain its own complex model of the situation? Under this scenario we would have opened up the possibility of the computer to bring forth its own answers. This leaves us to ask the question, are we starting to see the computer as part of our physical lives or is it still just a functional tool?

That's the crazy part! They have already become so much a part of our lives that there is no day that goes by without some interaction. We use some form of computer, or artificial intelligence in most everything we do. Examples of this are talking on the phone, starting your cars, looking at TV, cooking your food, they all are computerized these days. We use hand-held computers (i.e. I phone or androids), to Skype with other on the other side of the world.

Think about the banking and financial institutions, or hospitals, and the amount of data they use every day in answering questions about our health. Computers have become essential in every profession, from being used in open-heart surgeries, to going to the moon.

Computers carry out many functions from holding and storing data, which is necessary for our research and our inventions to helping doctors to perform a surgical procedure, via satellite. The process is endless!

The Internet

The internet has opened the world up to us, bringing us closer together. The influence of the internet has become so pervasive that we can no longer live the way we did twenty or thirty years ago. If we are not willing to use the computer, our lives can become quite a hardship.

Remember, years ago, when airlines introduced a new program that we needed to have a credit card to rent a car? Today this is just par for the course and we don't even think about it anymore. This is what Turing predicted: that machine intelligence (AI) would become so pervasive in our lives that we no longer see it as an invasion. The internet has integrated into all aspects of our lives from economy, education, and medicine, to finances, etc., and most people fail to even notice that it is present.

In "Computer World" newsletter dated November 2009, it was reported that research is being conducted on using the brain to control the computer in the near future. They stated that by the year 2020, we won't need a keyboard, or a mouse to control our computer. Instead, users will open documents and surf the web by using nothing more than their brain waves. Scientists at Intel's research lab in Pittsburgh are working to find ways to read and <u>harness human brain</u> *waves,* so they can be used to operate computers, television sets, and cell phones. The brain waves would be harnessed with sensors implanted in a person's brain.

The article went on to state that Andrew Chien, (vice president of research and director of future technologies research at Intel Labs), expressed that "he thought that human beings are remarkably adaptive." If we would have told people 20 years ago that they would be carrying around a computer all the time, we would have said that was crazy, and yet, it is our reality.

The article also reported that two years ago, scientists in the U.S. and Japan announced that a monkey's brain has been used to control a humanoid robot. Miguel Niclelis (a professor of neurobiology at Duke University who led the research on the project) said that this research was hopeful. He went on to say that this could possibly benefit paralyzed people in being able to walk again.

A few years ago, computers in schools were mostly used on a trial basis. However, today, one of the most effective methods of learning comes from the use of computers. While most schools are still not on the cutting edge of their use, it is impossible to deny the importance of a computer as an educational tool. Computers play an intricate role in all facets of education, as they do in many other spheres of our lives.

Communications

Communication is another area of technology which has brought a new twist of being able to translate a telephone conversations from one language to another. This is where we speak in English and our Japanese partners can hear and understand us, via a translation program. This has become quite commonly used for many language pairs today. It is also quite routine for a person with a cell phone to have this function as a part of his phone.

Internet communication today is primarily wireless, and routinely includes high-resolution images which allow for us to watch movies, use face-time, or you tube. There are also meetings and conferences being conducted all over the world, due to the internet communication. The internet allows us to reach out and touch someone on the other side of the world in seconds. Or do something as simple as locating the new restaurant a cross town.

Like most things there are always two sides to the story, and we need to keep our eye on the influences of the computer. We need to look at the roles it plays, and the importance we have given to this technology. By rendering so much value to this technology maybe we have deprived ourselves of our love connection.

Looking At The Influence

Wendell Wallach and Colin Allen in their book <u>The Moral Machine,</u> spoke of the ethical code in which they have chosen to be true. In the Code of Ethics of the National Society of Professional Engineers (NSPE), the first "fundamental canon" is that engineers shall "hold paramount the safety, health, and welfare of the public."

If giving machines moral standards would improve public welfare and safety, then it is upon the American engineers to feel their obligation to their own codes of ethics and to make the technology lead the way with moral understanding.

However, there is a bit of catch 22 in the principles of engineering itself. Its make-up is incrementally based (meaning it is formed from the past experiences), to make things better. This also means that they would have to look at the multi-dimensional process of values, and examine between the autonomy and sensitivity, to which they choose to place value. We must remember that given the idea of autonomy it does <u>not</u> give the blessing of sensitivity to us, it comes with its own structured value.

Just like life's journey, technology has its own journey, and it will always present us with its trade-offs. The simplest of tools has neither autonomy nor sensitivity. The computer cannot compose the letter without our input; the gun cannot harm our brother on its own! We need to continue to recognize and evaluate the value that computers bring to us. We must also recognize the value we have given to the tools, and how important we have made them to ourselves. The cell phone is a prime example of this technology. There have been many studies to express how it creates separation, rather than union, within families. This is illustrated by the amount of communication that takes place within any given family setting. Most of the parents I spoke with all stated this is a big topic in their household. Adults are not immune to this technology either, they find themselves no longer able to live without their cell phones. It is how they stay connected to the world.

Herein lies the power of social influence: believing that it is okay to <u>check</u>-<u>out</u>, and <u>not</u> be present. When we stop asking the question of ourselves (and of our society), about our values, then where will the value of our values come from? How can we accept or be at peace with the outcome of our actions (as co-creators) of our reality, when the observation of that reality has been obscured?

There is no doubt that the computer has made an impact on our social and physical lives that will never be changed. But we need to ask ourselves, have we turned off our connection, which allows us to recognize our love? Love needs to be shown (or shared) to be received; not only to others, but also by the willingness to show it to ourselves.

CHAPTER 4
Releasing Control

R eleasing control is about letting go of the illusions and all that comes with the idea of illusions. But it is extremely important that we recognize that we are functioning in a thought system of illusions. Most of our thoughts are but a projection of what we want in our tomorrow, or a reflection of a dream, or event, that happened in the past. These memories hold great value to us, which is why we hold onto them. But we must not forget that a projection is but a reflection of our illusions. To understand this can be quite simple actually, because there are only two choices to be made: one of <u>truth</u> and <u>love,</u> and the other of <u>fear</u> and <u>confusion</u>. We cannot choose both; or if we do, we will then believe that both sides can be seen as real. Illusions (by their nature) can never be real, because they are derived from fantasies— and this is always made from understanding.

The difficulty in releasing control comes from our conditioning, which is brought forth by the influence of our society, culture, and our parental teaching. The structure of social influences has affected every aspect of our lives. These influences have caused us to create behavior patterns and emotional reactions that have made us confused and fearful. Let us look at how students are acting out their confusion (in high school, and on college campuses across the country) and even around the world. They are but reflecting the confusion of their society as a whole, which is usually confused! Then, how can that society pass on anything other than its own confusion? Part of the process of any illusion is to make us believe that we know the answer, and this will always stop knowing from taking place. The knowing is a continuous process and will never stop—— this is part of nature's gift!

We have allowed our Illusions to tell us what the truth is, but, from only an intellectual point of view. But it has never been able to give us a clear example of what that truth is. It gives us only a tiny glimpse of what it should be, and then it would have us create the other part as a fantasy in our minds. Thus, allowing the fantasy to become truthful in our minds, and having us to accept it as our creation. We then tell ourselves that we are in control. This could have only one effect, which is for us to believe what we see is real and truthful to us.

This will then become our acknowledgment—— that we are in control! But (as I stated before) we can never receive a clear answer when we ask the question backwards. The ego will always asking its questions backward. What I mean by this is when we tell ourselves that we know the answer before the question is asked. Are when we tell ourselves what the outcome will be before it happens. This is what confusion and fear is, and what gives us the idea that we are in control.

Clarity cannot come from an illusion or fantasy, because they do <u>not</u> possess the capacity to be interchangeable. Nature, on the other hand, delivers truth and clarity in every step it takes— it puts it all right in front of us!

The dilemma is what part of our social influence do we question and which part do we choose to believe in? How much of the confusion are we willing to accept? Do we continue to buy that the illusions are real? Do we really believe that trying to control our brother's behavior has a meaningful end? Or, do we have the courage to ask if we really are in control? Then we must ask what are we afraid of (that is keeping us trapped in this continuous cycle). Until we welcome the answers to some of these questions, no real change can happen. We must be willing to relinquish the idea of <u>control</u>, to see that there is no need for it. Then we will realize to be afraid of our brothers, is to be afraid of ourselves.

We must welcome these questions with an open heart, for the truth to come in. By our willful invitation to love, we create no implied coercion. We welcome the response of the universal way, and will gladly use nature's way to our clarity. Any other approach requires the influence from outside of us, and must be based on our past or the future and <u>neither</u> of these can ever reflect the truth now.

They can only reflect the influences of our yesterday, or the projections of our desires for tomorrow. The past is gone and will never return. However, if we choose to keep it alive, we must give it our power, and bring it to the present. This brings yesterday alive today, and this can only happen if we have created an illusion— and made it real. Yet, this is the path that many of our brothers and sisters are following every day, and believing that they are in control.

We need to ask the question of ourselves: am I <u>really</u> about love or do I just <u>talk</u> about <u>love</u>? If we are still thinking that we are in control, we have <u>not</u> yet found the key to love. Love is not about control, but about having a connection and union with our feeling of oneness. This allows us to recognize that they are one in the same (at a spiritual level), and are never in conflict——so there will be no need for control.

We will then start to see the clarity, where we once saw only confusion, and this will become a great confidence booster. Clarity will always speak for itself and help us stay the course. To be able to stay the course also requires us to have faith. Our confusion is but a reflection of the illusions, which are of our <u>own</u> making. Our teachers and scholars alike have told us what truth is, and yet this has not held up over the years——as truthful!

Regardless of who is saying it, if it is falling apart or does not reflect clarity, why would we want to hold onto it? If we find ourselves with two answers to the same question, we could not have clarity, only an opinion. This could only mean that we have been confused on that subject. So, how could we have truth? Scholars have told us that there are many truths, and that we must have an open mind about these things. They show us only a glimpse of truth, and want us to follow it, when there is always much confusion.

Even in our own family tree there has been much confusion about the subject of truth, not because our parents did not love us. This happen because they were conditioned to bring forth the same illusions of their own experiences that they were told and believed were love and truthful.

This is the framework of society and political groups in general. Their mechanism is to control the group, and we are a part of that group. Our parents did not understand what they were being told. They just went along with what they were told, and wanting the approval of friends, family, and to hold to their relationship in general—— because this was just the way it was done.

Social Control

Social control refers to societies and political mechanisms or processes that regulate individual and group behavior. This process has led us to conformity and compliance of the rules given by society, state, or social group. It also has been passed on from father- to -son and from family-to-family, and throughout our culture. Until we wake up and realize what we have a chosen, we will continue to be followers. Here are very important questions to ask ourselves, in trying to understand the idea of control:

- What do I control?
- How do I control anything?
- What do I have control of?
- If I recognize my spiritual self, do I have a need for the idea or the perception of control?

What do I really control? As I asked this question in my survey the most immediate response was, yes, they control a lot of things. However, as they started to look at some of the questions more closely, they realized there were very few things that they actually controlled. This brought on some interesting thoughts about control, and more confusion. We then had to accept that we are not in control —and this can be quite fearful! Most of us walk with a great deal of fear and uncertainty about our tomorrow, which leads us into a continuous state of doubt.

When we look at the idea of control closely we realize what we come to understand is that we are just observing an event that has already taken place. Therefore, the idea of control is all about regulation, comparing and commanding a particular direction or outcome. How can we control something that is always in constant flux? That means for us to control a situation, we would have to constantly be willing to change our mind about what just happened. In hope of controlling the outcome, thus making it fit what we want it to be. A changing value of this magnitude would have <u>no</u> real value to us at all—or would it?

Created Values

A real important question is, have we over valued the things in our lives? How do we open the door to understand what it is that we truly value? The real value of anything is to understand its meaning, which is given to us by the experience itself. However, to receive this gift, we must be willing to receive the experience or "take it in" and this can be uncomfortable sometimes. It is important that we don't become trapped by what we wanted to happen. But to allow ourselves the experience to understand what just took place.

This often means to open the door to some uncomfortable feelings, and to accept and understand that these feelings are okay. Often, if we are uncomfortable, we are <u>not</u> trying to control the situation or outcome. We are just letting things take their natural course. We must realize that when we are ready to open this door in our own hearts, we are ready to become receivers. We will then allow ourselves to experience the blessing of that moment, and this is where true value lies.

If we allow ourselves this opportunity, to accept the moment without judgment, we will truly receive its blessing. It is only in confusion and chaos that we become separate, and then create the need to control. But, when we can find acceptance, it is usually absent of separation or control, then our awareness and values will be different. However, to <u>accept</u> this new value means to surrender to the experience and join <u>with</u> it, thereby becoming "one" with the experience. Here lies the truth and understanding of our value and blessings.

Often, from our experiences, clarity is revealed, and then we are able to recognize there is no need to be in control. With this clarity we realize that most event are <u>not</u> controllable, only manageable. This is due to the dynamic of time itself, which we are not in control of! We can only manipulate time, not control it! What is obvious needs no control. What would be the value in creating an internal conflict or fight with ourselves or others? This could only create more separation with our spirit. Regardless of what story we tell ourselves, our actions to attack or to be separate are never about love— they are about our fears.

It is important that we understand that we do not attack what we love. This idea of a love-hate relationship does <u>not</u> exist. That is like saying that darkness and light can coexist— they cannot! Love cannot have a dark side! This does not mean that the persons we care about cannot affect us or even hurt us. They can, but we must always look first at their <u>intent</u> <u>of</u> <u>heart</u> to evaluate the true value of love.

This will always leave room for compassion and forgiveness to operate in our hearts. When we let the energy of our heart receive the energy of our partner's, we have allowed ourselves to experience (or accept) what just happened truthfully. Then a union is created, and we can feel the pain and suffering of our partner without a misunderstanding. I believe to harm someone else would be to harm ourselves, and there is no love in that.

Developing A New Belief System

We often think we need to control our outcome for many different reasons. Some of them we are aware of, and some are conditional responses. For most of us these reactions come from the use of our frequency and patterns, brought forth by our conditioning. However, in some cases our response is about wanting to be right or in control. Often, this happens because of our conditioning and belief system, rather than the way things really are.

Quite often we can recognize that other people's cruel acts are a form of conditioning. Unfortunately, our conditioning is so powerful that most people follow the approach they are most familiar with (even when they feel that something is wrong). However, they choose not to ask questions, they just continue to do what they have always done, even though it could be harmful to themselves and others.

But, often our conditioning is so over-powering it clouds our judgment, and has us search for the need to be right, or in control. This is what creates and drive our action "to harm." Have we become so entrenched in our ways that we fear the possibility of change? Are we afraid to change? If we cannot look at these questions with an open heart we will have no choice but to continue with a foundation of weakness. When will it stop? When will we wake up and realize that this is not the way of love or unity, and will not bring us peace?

It is imperative that we start to ask some of these questions about our conditioning, in order for us to understand our blessings.

To look upon the Godliness within us, we will need to recognize the soundness of our foundation— and this will lead us to the "truth." This truth was given to us as a <u>birthright.</u> Truth is eternal just like we are, and cannot be altered or changed. This truth is always right in front of us. We all have been given the gift of unity and love, but we often chosen to deny it, for the need to be right or in control instead. This means the idea of being right has become more valuable to us. This happens because we want to see only with our physical eyes, which often deceive us, and show us illusions. If we can learn to trust "Our Godly" approach, we will see the truth is always revealed, and is always right-in-front-of- us.

Have you ever thought of yourself in a "Godly way"? It would stand to reason, in order to think this way, we would want to hear the "Godly-voice" within us. This requires us to take in the information necessary to recognize our "Godly-self." If we continue to deny this information, we will be denying a part of ourselves, which most often does not lead to a peaceful outcome. It is imperative that we allow ourselves to surrender to this Godly voice before we can move forward to develop a new thought-system. However, if we choose to move too fast, or be too early, that could be a recipe for disaster.

We must give ourselves time, to ask, "What is our blessing of this event?" We will then be amazed at what will be revealed to us! A couple of things happen when we start to ask questions of ourselves. One thing is that we become more mindful of the event, and to the circumstances around us. This means that we have chosen to face our fears, and to approach the chaos and confusion head on. Secondly, is when we decide to be mindful of ourselves we surrender, and take in the whole event. We are then able to see its real value and truth. Then, in this moment, reality is revealed to us, and with this recognition— clarity is born!

We must be willing to recognize what has just been unveiled without judgment or the need to control or to be right. Because in our confusion we do <u>not</u> understand what is right. We must be willing to surrender to our Godly selves, in order to find clarify and truth. The blessings we receive all come with particular circumstances that are unique to that moment. This recognition and clarity will come with a sound understanding, and only at that moment can it be revealed. However, it is imperative that we are willing to surrender to the moment for a new belief system to be developed.

What Do We Really Know?

What do we really know, anyway? If we think about it, most of the things that happen around us are seen from our past, or represent a projection we are making into the future. We don't create the event we see——we are merely observers of it! Being a good observer means we must be willing to see the whole event (from start to finish), allowing us to have a clear understanding of what really happened.

How often have we seen only a small amount of an event or situation, and yet we go on to tell ourselves we know the outcome? Is this really the outcome that is being revealed, or merely the one we would have chosen to see (created out of our own illusions)? If we choose an outcome and did not observe it, can this be the truth? Or, is this just the source of our confusion, and telling ourselves what we want it to be? Wouldn't this be an illusion? Truth can only reflect the whole, and is always right for <u>all</u> concerned, and will <u>not</u> just benefit a few.

Blessings, by their nature, always serve the whole. They could not serve only a few and be a blessing. Blessings are there to enhance us, even though they can be painful or come with a bit of suffering sometimes. When we can see the blessings, the pain and suffering will always fade to the background because we will no longer be confused by the value we have placed upon them. The pain will then be seen as a means to our growth, and that will be received as a meaningful part of our journey. A quote by Rumi "The cure for pain is in pain." Another example of this is childbirth I was told that it can be quite painful. However, many of the women I spoke with said that when they were given their baby after the delivery they no-longer thought about the pain.

We must always recognize who the messenger is. The ego wants us to believe only what our eyes show us, but, far too often, they do not reflect reality or the whole truth. We must also understand that the messenger is both the <u>sender</u> and <u>receiver</u>. If we believe that all that we are is just our bodies, then we must believe the illusions are real, and give them great value. Until we can appreciate the idea of our Godliness, we will accept our conditioning as a sound approach, which has led us down the wrong path. A path where illusions appear to be real—and confusion is the order of the day. We need to recognize and accept that we cannot make this journey alone. Our unity is what makes real whole, and it represent union—— not separation.

To attack our brothers or sisters is to believe that they are different at a spiritual level. However, this difference is expressed only in what our eyes show us. It will also have us believe in illusions and to accept the separation as a sound direction. Only if we share in the illusion does it become real. If we hold our focus on our brother's innocence, then we can touch it, because this is a necessary step for us to recognize our own innocence.

To know means that we must understand our own journey, and to realize that we are not alone in our union. We could not have arrived where we are without the help and guidance of others. It is important that we recognize that in our <u>union,</u> we come to know our <u>whole</u>-<u>self</u>, and to realize that we are not alone. Our union is the blessing on our journey, and we need to register that unity with each and every person we meet.

Identifying With Our Spirit

"Sameness" speaks volumes to the idea of union, and to the fact that we are all one in spirit. We need to let go of the idea of <u>Me</u> or <u>Mine</u>, or that "<u>I</u>" approach in taking our next step. It is important that we recognize how to love ourselves, so we can forgive ourselves and others. Being able to recognize the illusions for what they really are will help us to understand that confusion is but a poor perception of what just happened. If we allow ourselves to be <u>patient</u> (and trust our "Godly self"), the truth of any event or circumstance will present itself.

When we can feel the blessing of that moment, we will start to see clearly as we move from chaos to clarity. By us not giving into the ego's confusion, and choosing not to attack (but to love instead), we will feel the union of our oneness. When we accept the fear or confusion of any illusion we have chosen to identify with it, and have thus made the confusion or illusion real. If we can never realize our own internal concealment, we will continue to hide from ourselves. And continue to accept the false reality, because we believe it is real. This approach will always keep us in the dark about our true reality, and keep us believing that the illusions are real.

To look upon our true reality is to recognize or understand our "Holy purpose," which is to recognize that we are spirits. Which helps us to understand our blessing, and the meaning of the holy instant! Our patience allows us to recognize the clarity of that moment, and then we become aware of the blessings that are being revealed.

All of our experiences are there for our growth, on some level. However, we need to forgo the temptation of being right or to be in control for the blessings to be revealed. Remember, we are but observers of time—— not the controller of it. To understand and accept that the truth is always there, (right in front of us), we must be willing to allow ourselves to be the observer of what it is we see. Then, our fear will disappear, because we have added light to where there was only darkness. But, we must first mustard up the courage to "enter the room" before the fear will disappear. Once we have confronted our fear and confusion, we will recognize that we are the <u>source</u> of our fear—— and our courage is our light that remove them. Where there is light darkness cannot be or exist.

Confusion comes with many different faces, so we must be continuously vigilant of what we choose to call real. The ego can be quite deceptive in how it presents its story. It will have us believe that we can <u>alter</u> the truth, and that it can still remain truthful. This will make us question our direction (or create doubt), and this will make us feel uncomfortable in trusting ourselves and others. How often have we researched a project, and been very committed to accomplishing our task, when a friend tells us that this is a crazy idea, and that it is not possible. Then, before long, we have given up on our dream or project.

If we are the *means and the source that* set the goal, would it not be logical to think that we would be <u>given</u> the means to accomplish it? And yet, for many of us the goals are never finished. Herein lies the deception of our ego: never wanting us to see our true self or accomplish any goal. This is because the ego does not know the "truth." It only thinks about truth, in the form of illusion or fantasies. To know truth, we must be willing to wait on its arrival, rather than to tell ourselves that we are the creator of it.

However, if we would allow ourselves a regular dose of patience, and move with an open heart, truth will be revealed. We will then start to understand the depth of our love for ourselves, and the oneness we share with others. This will allow us to see with a different vision; and not just with our physical eyes, (which we share with our ego), but with our internal sight. This approach would allow us to see without the judgment. Learning to see with our internal vision gives us a different level of thought and perception about what was revealed. In that <u>spiritual</u> <u>instant,</u> we will have clarity of our purpose and journey.

Recognizing Our Confusion

Recognizing our confusion means that we are willing to ask some of life's important questions. Like, what is it that we believe in? What is it that we really know? By looking at how we answer these questions, we actually begin to realize what we really do not know. Then we can look back at what our parents have told us, and question how much of it is really the truth, or is it just more information passed on? We should ask ourselves if we believe in the idea of Sin. Does sin alter our reality? Is (sin) or guilt ever justified? Do we have Faith, and if so, in what? Do we believe that sin and error are the same? Does confusion produce fear inside of us? How solid is our foundation in who we believe we are? What is it that we feel certain about? Do we feel connected to something other than ourselves? We must address many of these questions in order for us to recognize, or to have a clear understanding of who we are. This will enable us to not be terrified of what we may discover.

One of the most important things for us to realize is that our body has no feelings of its own, and that it takes all it direction from our thoughts. This can be quite reassuring when we can accept that we are the source of our being, and this will always go beyond our body. Recognizing this can remove the poor perception in our evaluation of ourselves. Allowing us to no longer accept the illusions—— as our reality.

We are the transmitters of the feelings that we want to have. Neuroscience tells us that we feel certain electrical impulses moving through our bodies, and this makes physical responses possible. If we were not confused, then we would be able to see and recognize "truth." Our bodies and minds are always in a state of flux. We know this because of our fragmented thoughts and the poor choices we make about our direction. This creates a conflict of sorts, because "How can we receive the love of our brother when we cannot see him as he is?"

Our confusion will always have us focus our attention on the body, rather than on the union or spirit. This will make our direction not about the betterment of mankind, but only about our personal interest. Our fragmented way of thinking will never allow us to feel at peace, or to know truth. So, it is imperative that we start to ask the question *"Have We Lost Our Spiritual Connection?"* if we are in search of <u>peace</u>. From this peace the truth is revealed, and we had nothing to do with it—— acceptance is all that is required. There is no fight in acceptance, and without a fight, there is no fear or confusion. That which is clear cannot be confusing. It is important that we recognize that we are the source of our light, and this is <u>not</u> our bodies!

The body is but a medium, and, like any medium, it is a means for us to receive information. The body is a receiver and sender of messages, which are given to us to view our experiences. The medium can <u>not</u> be the source of us; it can only be the means. We must question our inner-self, so we may clear-up the distortion about our source. However, if we do not want to know about this part of ourselves, we will continue to deny its presence (our spirit). By doing this we will have chosen the direction of confusion. Then, we can be quite confused by our own actions sometimes, because in many situations our actions makes no sense and have no logical foundation. This often leaves us to wonder why we choose this particular direction in the first place.

Most of our messages are sent by only one source and yet, both our Holy Spirit and our ego are aware of that source's center. It is highly believed that our physical body is governed by the physical realm, and our egos control this domain. It is also important that we become aware of our spiritual side, to keep us from choosing the direction of pain and suffering. We were never told how to do this so we keep making the same mistakes over and over again.

However, a mindful approach is the answer we have been looking for—— to be at peace, and not to suffer with confusion. If we have made the choice to accept love, joy, peace, as our direction, then the other choices of hatred, judgments, and vengeance will no longer have any appeal. The ego's energy is always projecting outwardly in hopes of being received by its next victim or prey. And this could only bring about more separation and confusion, and not union.

Source Of Confusion

If we cannot look upon ourselves and see a complete person (total in every regard), then we must be seeing ourselves as a fragmented element of the whole. This will bring on confusion for us, because we cannot see our whole self. If we use this approach to help us feel good about what we <u>do</u> and see, we will continue to create substitutions. This allows us to recognize the fragment as whole, and to give value because it is what we have created. However, from that point forth, the reality of our vision will always be in question. Because a fragment can never reflect the whole.

There would no longer be consistency or clarity in our thoughts. Certainty would have faded and died, and doubt would have become the order of the day. Illusions are but fantasies, and can never replace the "truth." However, these illusions take on many forms, and if we choose to accept the illusion as our direction we must take on all that comes with the illusion. With this kind of thought process, we will walk around "consciously-unconscious," and this will affect every step of our journey. And we will not feel peace or joy in our lives.

Only when we are willing to make changes to what we see in front of us have we chosen to accept a new and different reality. To see something other than what is in front of us would mean we were willing to alter reality for our own purpose. But to create a false reality is to make a substitution to the reality that is in front of us. This substitution allows us to believe what we see is real, and tells us that we are in control. The question is, "Can we alter or create our own reality from a fragment?"

We often make substitutions because it gives us the feeling of being in control. Then we tell ourselves that this is pleasurable and real. But let us look at how often we've thought we knew what we wanted or needed, and later realized that there was no pleasure derived from it. How can we choose to alter truth to derive pleasure, when it is clear that we are uncertain as to what truth is?

Fragmented by our poor understanding of truth, how can we use this process to serve the whole? A fragmented thought can only see a small and limited part of the whole. And often we allow this tiny fragment to become enormous, and hold our focus on our differences, rather than recognizing our oneness and wholeness.

A friend recently asked me, why is it so hard to make the necessary changes to see the other person, with love? I responded that we are focusing on the fragment, and not the whole. We must learn to see with the <u>one</u> direction of love that is within us all, then we will be able to recognize this love in others. This is where we should learn to hold our focus, then change will becomes easy. When we make substitutions to our life (and to our stories), we have chosen to deny what is there in front of us. Whatever is there is <u>not</u> there by accident. Remember, we are only a small part of what it is we see. We must remember we are only here to be a <u>receiver</u> of the experience, and hopefully be <u>awakened</u> by it. Herein lies the proper use of the experience, and of time itself. However, to alter it even in the slightest of ways is to believe that we know best, and tell ourselves what it should be. This is but a projection of our desires for tomorrow, rather than allowing ourselves to receive the moment.

Every experience comes with its own blessings. We all like to pursue our dreams and goals in hopes of the joy and happiness they may bring. However, sometimes this doesn't take place. Let us look at some of the reasons as to why not. If our thoughts are fragmented, then wouldn't it stand to reason that our line-of-thinking would be clouded and confused? This will <u>not</u> allow us to pursue a clear line of logic, for us to accomplish our goals.

This is possible because a fragmented mind will usually follow the path of confusion and fear. Fear, (by its definition) brings forth a lack understanding, and will normally produce more confusion and illusions. Most of our dreams are but our fantasies, and have no logical foundation to be pursued. They are completely unaware of clarity or truth.

To be aware of clarity or truth we must willing to embrace our faith. This pair are never separate. Where one is, the other will always be, and has always been.

Having Faith

Faith is a critical part in our search for peace, and to release the idea of control. However, to lack faith is to deny or believe that we know best. In either case, we have chosen a different reality over the one that is in front of us. The instant we choose a new reality, our body will do everything in its power to make it real for us. This will constantly create problems for us, because this will make these changes truth. This would have us treat <u>certainty</u> as though it were a bad thing. The fact of the matter is, if we have a lack of faith, what we see will make us quite confused.

Having faith is nothing more than a conscious choice to surrender to what is right in front of us.

Faithlessness is to make substitutions and create illusions Instead of accepting the reality that was revealed. However, if we have brought along fear and illusions as our travelling partner, we will always look upon what we see with distortion and doubt. This is the thought process of <u>faithlessness</u>, which comes with uncertainty and doubt. But on the other hand, faith and truth always come with certainty.

It is important that we realize the truth is real, and is always right in front us! How can we evaluate the truth if we remove or alter the situation? It would be unfair if we tried to make changes to what is not there. This would take things out of context in our evaluating the truth and just create more confusion.

How could we ever find reconciliation in this approach? Can a situation ever be reconciled if we are willing to make substitution or replacement to its present condition? Any time we are willing to make changes to the facts, we must ask ourselves if we are really interested in the truth.

Faith is a belief in something, or a willingness to receive an outcome which is beyond what our eyes show us. There are no words to describe faith as a definition; it is a connection to a deeper part of us. Faith is a connection which brings with it peace and love, and this goes beyond the desires of our dreams. It helps us understand our brothers and recognizes our spirit.

Acknowledging Our New Path

Acknowledging this fact brings us closer to the "Godliness" by giving us an <u>awareness</u> of a deeper part of ourselves. To deny our

Godly presence within us is to create fear and confusion. To accept anything (regardless of what it may be), on some level we need to acknowledge it as real. This means we must believe in what we have accepted or created. Perhaps, a more important question we should be asking is, "Did we create what we just saw, or are we merely the observer of it?" However, with a closer evaluation, we come to realize that we control very few things!

Let us look at how often the things we planned and did these things turn out as we planned them? This could also imply that our skill for planning is not very good, or that we do not do very many things with accuracy. It is important for us to remember that time is only there for us, to use or manipulate, but it is not under our controll. We often take the things we see and call them our own, believing that this gives us control. And with all the changes taking place around us, how could this not make us confused–when there is always a constant stream of new data in our path. We must stay mindful just to keep up, so we may have a clear point of view. By approaching things with a point of view of open mindedness we realize that we are just observers of our reality. With this understanding we can start to see that there is no real effort necessary on our part to see the experience, for what it brings.

When we allow ourselves the opportunity to <u>feel</u> (rather than think), and <u>accept</u> (rather than control) we will then be acknowledging our new path with faith. Then the more we will learn to surrender to the feeling, of our <u>spiritual</u> <u>connection,</u> and our union.

Our Purpose

We all set goals and make plans in hopes our futures will be fulfilling. Our plans are normally a good thing if they represent the betterment of the planet, as a foundational part of our thought-system. Our purpose should be of one-mindedness, and should carry a pure, **intent of heart**. And this process must be driven by love, itself, for there is no other which can carry the spirits of our brothers and sisters around the world. Our first choice must always be one of <u>love</u>, to demonstrate true purpose of our actions.

We must understand that <u>love</u> is <u>not</u> just a word, but a series of <u>actions</u> that requires our <u>participation</u> for it to exist.

To recognize this is to state that love cannot be partial and must represent the whole. This can only be possible if "the whole" is implied to be <u>complete,</u> and lacks nothing for its joy. If we can recognize such a state of love in ourselves, then we will have an <u>equal</u> love for our brothers. How could this not be received as being a beautiful and loving action?

However, we look at the situation that we find ourselves in on a daily basis, and realize that we walk with a lot of fear. This confused state leads to feelings of anger and violence——and the list can go on and on. I am always amazed that we are not willing to step back and look at the situation from a different point of view. Remember, there is always a different point of view, and we need to acknowledge both for a clear evaluation of what happened. This allows us to understand our purpose and our intent-of-heart.

I would have you to ask this question, "Can we make an informed decision with only partial information and still believe that we can have a fair and just outcome?" If our purpose does not include the well-being of the universe, isn't there something missing in our intent of heart, and our purpose? Love is whole and complete in its being just as we are whole in ours. To understand this statement will allow us to feel this love and know that we are fulfilling our purpose when we share this love. Our intent of heart will always reflects our purpose, because we cannot fake our intent; it either has purity, or it doesn't.

Sometimes, we can all act like children with our innocence of not understanding the truth. This can also make us act out with foolishness, or cruelty toward others sometimes. We must not focus on just the physical acts we played out, but to look at the innocence, or the spirit of our brothers, and to allow ourselves to be forgiving. If we are able to recognize this innocence in others, we must have unveiled it to ourselves, as well.

With this recognition, we start to realize that we are not alone and have never been alone. And realize there is strength in not being alone, regardless of how big or small the crowed. When we start to feel the clarity of our unity, it will be quite comforting to us. This will bring about a feeling of continuous love. In our innocence, we will recognize our oneness. However, if we cannot recognize our purpose, then we cannot see our innocence or the source or union. This will only allow us to see only the choices of difference and separation, and then have us produce more fear and confusion. Thus never recognizing our true purpose, which is to love, and the willingness to share love.

Losing Sight Of Our Spiritual Self

Our spiritual-self, is not to be looked upon as our bodies that we have been taught to cherish. It's about creating a living relationship with our Creator. Our physical bodies only give us the right to be co-creator, but the greater part of us is <u>not</u> (and never has been) our bodies or the physical realm. We must recognize that material things can wither away and decay and therefore cannot be eternal, and do not reflect the spirit of our Godliness.

We were all given the right to co-create, and, yes, we create things all the time. But these things we create are just idols, and they never last. We have made these substitutions and things, and have chosen them over the love of others. But, no idol can share its intent-of-heart, because it cannot feel. There can be no true relationship with an object, or a thing that has no real value to share.

Yet, we cherish and love these things and idols over our brothers. The person that chooses <u>not</u> to love, becomes the perfect host for destruction or for hatred and confusion. This is the ego domain and it thrives on the power we feed it. The ego <u>wants</u> the idols, and the relationships we create with them, because to the ego there are no attachments to anything. Its purpose is to satisfy its needs for more chaos and confusion, and to persuade us to move off the course of love.

Could it be that we have lost sight of the purpose to our journey? This will have us focus more on the goals or projects, rather than our joy of the journey. Our focus has become clouded, and we are not be able to recognize our purpose. We need to take time to nourish our spiritual-self, and try to understand our true self. It is important that we know that we are more than our bodies, and the objects or things we created. Look at all the things we see without our eyes; knowing that your best friend needs a call on a particular day, or having the right answer when we are not supposed to know the answer, or showing up at mom's house when she just fell. We just take it all for granted, because we have lost sight of our own <u>insightfulness</u> that we are all "Godly" and connected!

For many of us we have come a long way in understanding that we are greater than our bodies. And yet, for some of us, we are quite confused by the idea that we are more than our bodies. Confused, because when we look around at the relationships we see, and there is often little love being shown. This proves to us that bodies, of themselves, cannot create love, and are unable to choose a direction of their own accord that bring about love.

Love has to be greater than just the <u>idea</u> of love. Most of us function with merely the idea of love. We then find it very hard to give-in to love, without a list of criteria of what we want it to be. If we have a list for what love is to be, then love must be taking place somewhere else, because it is not right in front of us. Then it must be looking at the idea of love and this cannot be love.

Remember love needs <u>no</u> list to be expressed. However, the <u>idea</u> of love will always come with a list.

The most important thing to remember about love is that <u>it needs our presence to exist.</u> We must be a <u>welcoming</u> participant— for love to take place. If we are absent, so too will love be. This is where confusion stems from—believing that illusions can represent love. This can become our trap if we believe that love comes from <u>outside</u> of us (which is impossible), but we often are searching for love in the wrong place. This is what I meant by losing sight of our spiritual-self!

Let us look at all the ways we try to find love, and all the things we do and all the sacrifices we make, so that someone will love us. We have often told ourselves how important our appearance is for us to be loved. All the things we have done to fit in with the group to be loved. How often have we changed our mind to be accepted by others? All of these are just another point of view and seen from the physical side of our being, which carries a long list of conditions that are necessary for us to fit in.

If love comes from outside of us, then it would have to be influenced by our feelings, rather than our thoughts. The influences that come from our physical realm are forever changing, and without any regard to balance or certainty to their outcome. By using such an approach, will we ever find love or our spiritual-connection or just more confusion and illusions? This will always leave us feeling lost and alone with no idea of our connection.

Accepting Our Blessings

Accepting does not mean that we must have a clear understanding of the things that are taking place around us. But it does mean that we should be at peace with who we are, and the outcome we produced. The process of acceptance is about allowing ourselves the right to ask the question, "What are we supposed to learn from this experience." "Or how can we grow from what just happened?" By choosing to ask these questions, we have given ourselves a way to receive the experience and welcome its results.

This is very important before we are able to evaluate a true outcome. We need to feel what just happened and to allow ourselves to take in the experience. When we do this there is no need to make a judgment. Then, our blessings will be revealed. By allowing ourselves the experience we have allowed us to be the receiver of the whole picture. However, if we see merely a glimpse, and believe we have seen the whole picture, we can only have a distorted view. Then we will find ourselves looking at a fragment, and mistakenly referring to it as the whole.

We need the <u>whole</u> experience to receive the blessing. Our blessing is never fragmented; but it may come to us in a fragment form due to our lack of understanding. If we have clarity of our situation, we can see the love in what just took place. Even if it means that we were hurt or injured physically or emotionally in the process. We will come to understand that the hurt or anguish we feel would be part of the experience, and we would be perfectly willing to accept the outcome.

We must recognize that clarity and understanding bring no fear or conflict. The more we are able to surrender to the experience without judgment, the more we realize that we are <u>not</u> the creator of our reality but just the <u>observer</u> of it. And as an observer, we are merely taking in the data— not creating it. This is our purpose (to take in the data) and the blessings that come with it. Surrendering to the inner-voice means to learn to trust a new-found way of thinking. This will help us to release the idea that we are controlling that moment. Then, we will start to see with a different vision, and not so much with our eyes— but with the vision of our Godliness. However, this requires that we surrender to the spirit of us, and not to the body of us.

It is important for us to accept that we are "Godly" people, and that we are to embrace love and goodness as part of our natural being. We must be willing to recognize this trait, so that we may see this same trait in our brothers. Realizing they, too, must be "Godly" as well.

Acceptance requires very little of us generally. It only asks that we don't try to make what we see real by adding something that is not there. One of the critical parts of <u>acceptance</u> is to allow ourselves to receive the gift, without judgment or adjustment of any kind. This can become difficult if we tell ourselves that we understand or know the outcome of what is going to happen——with only a fragment of information. This will always foster fear and confusion. This will set up an internal fight and conflict within and one we cannot win. Whenever we attack on any level, our logical filter will do all that is in its power to make what we have done real to us.

Once we have accepted that spiritual part of ourselves (as to who we are), then we will see that we are far more than just our physical body. Acceptance does require us to have a bit of <u>faith</u> in our "spiritual-self" in order to be comfortable with the idea of acceptance.

But faith (much like our spirit) is <u>outside</u> the scope of our conditioning and patterns that we have been taught. This might make surrendering (to some of us) quite difficult. This is because faith requires so little from us we want to add our little part to the equation to make it better.

Faith is not about doing something. Instead, faith is about <u>receiving</u> something. This requires only that we be willing to receive the gift of the experience. To accept the experience with an absent of judgment is to recognize a new thought-system that we don't understand. By allowing ourselves to be okay with <u>not</u> understanding what just happened, we open the door to <u>receiving</u>. With this recognition we can merely ask, "What did I just experience?" We then look upon our blessings for they will always be right in front of us. However, we cannot determine their meaning until we have received the total experience. Allowing our light to shine within will bring forth the clarity and understanding of our experience—— thus, giving us a miracle which is beyond our control.

Being cannot be defined by the past, present or future, it just is. Being transcends time itself, thus cannot be defined by time. This is our blessing!

CHAPTER 5
The Journey Back

*T*o love ourselves is to heal ourselves, and we must see the whole in order to be healed. To accomplish this, we must be able to recognize our oneness, because the whole can only reflect itself.

A few years ago, I started to wonder how I could reconnect with my spiritual self. Then I wondered what does that really mean? I intellectually thought I knew what it meant, but as I pondered the thought deeper, I realized that my scope of this subject was quite shallow and confusing.

How do we determine our spiritual understanding? Does this understanding come from our parents, religion, society, or does it come as a natural gift? Looking at these factors they all come with our cultural make-up, and their own level of confusion.

Then I asked what is it that makes us spiritual in the first place? When all of the ideas just mentioned are but methods, we were told and taught. And none of these concepts or methods will get us to a place that allows us to reconnect. They cannot take us to a place where enlightenment takes place, or where love is shared.

And yet this is what I believe our spiritual connection is about. Yes, there are many who have tried (and a few who have succeeded) in helping to change our direction to accomplish the task of loving ourselves. People like Jesus Christ, Buddha, Mother Teresa, Mahatma Gandhi, Martin Luther King Jr. , Thich Nhat Hanh (just to name a few), have all given us a clear picture to follow over the years. However, most of us have chosen to use our social conditioning as our method of choice. This method has moved us forward with only what we were told is joyous and peaceful, but we never really understood it.

Until we take a close look at this statement and understand its meaning, we will continue to believe what we have been told about our joy and to what we call truthful. We often feel the need to change direction, but we stay on the old course because of our conditioning, because we fear change. So, when we realize that the task is harder than we thought, we often are willing to "throw in the towel." Usually, we find ourselves accepting the advice of others that tells us the task cannot be accomplished. And we actually believe them, and throw in the towel.

But the reality is that difficulty is nothing more than another task before us; an opportunity to grow and nothing more. It is just another moment in time for us to see with a different set of eyes and to make a spiritual connection. We must recognize the wholeness that we are, which allows us to connect with our spiritual self. And this will allow us to hear our inner-voice!

However, our conditioning will often dim our view, or soften our inner-voice, which creates a sense of lack in our understanding. This makes us feel fearful to change and to seek our true purpose. We need to trust our <u>inner-voice</u>, and start to believe in the oneness of ourselves, which is critical to our journey back. Our clarity and understanding is within us, and has always been there. We need only to make our spiritual connection. But we often choose to deny its presence, and we make valuable what we have been told instead.

Choosing New Direction

In the evaluation of the new direction we have chosen, we must look at the thought-system we use to make that choice. When taking our decisions apart, we must realize there are only two major thought-systems that are available for us to use.

- First one is that of love and peace
- And the second is that of fear and confusion

The first system is the one of Love and Peace. It is given to us by nature, and follows the universal laws. These laws (by their nature) will not permit contradictions. However, the other system we use is created by our own ego. It comes with fear and confusion, and is not natural. Both thought-systems are consistent in their desire to have our allegiance. These two <u>methods</u> are diametrically opposed in all respects. We can never reconcile our actions by moving from one to the other. The one thought-system which is given by our Creator brings forth clarity and understanding. The other system is created by our own ego and our social conditioning that leaves us with fear and confusion. In making our choice about which system we use we must either accept the idea that we are in control or surrender to what is natural.

We know that all journeys must have a destination and purpose. Yet, we so often go to a particular place with no clear understanding as to why we are going there. But later realize that we move without a destination or purpose often creating a meaningless journey. Choosing our direction gives purpose and meaning for our existence; and a reason for us to go forward. If our direction has purpose it will give us the necessary focus to accomplish the task at hand. This in turn, gives us the necessary energy to take on whatever comes our way as a part of our journey. If we can learn to do this, we will come to understand the process of acceptance. And this will be the start of our journey back.

This only requires a willingness to believe that the truth is always within us, and only needs us to surrender to it—— for it to be revealed. This can be a hard concept to understand. Because for most of our lives, we have been told to believe in only what we can see. However, to surrender is about faith, which we cannot seen.

This then can become quite confusing for us, sometimes, because our eyes show us <u>illusions </u>all the time. Spiritually, truth is our inheritance, given to us by God (our Creator), as a never-ending process. We only need to surrender to it, to know that it is real.

Question: One of my patients asked why is it so hard for most of us accept our internal vision? I shared with him that we must learn first to surrender to be able to accept this internal sight. We must first be willing to acknowledge that we have been given another form of vision. Sight other than the physical sight of our eyes. We have all seen many things without the sight of our physical eyes. We do this all the time. For example, most inventions have come from the sight of our internal vision. Think of all the things that we have seen in our mind's eye, and that we never really saw with our physical eyes, and yet we know they are real. This in many cases has allowed us to be sound in our choices and our direction.

This is because God (our Creator) has given us this vision, which goes <u>beyond</u> our physical sight. So, we may be able to recognize truth and clarity as the natural way. Because when we use only our eyes for evaluation we often lose sight of clarity. It is imperative that we question the <u>clarity</u> of our vision, to determine the <u>truth</u> of it. Truth has been given to us as our <u>birthright</u>. However, we must be willing to invite our Creator in— to receive this truth! This truth and clarity will bring forth an understanding and faith. What better partner to have on our long journey back— than faith!

Clear Purpose

We must understand that our journeys are <u>not</u> without purpose or meaning. All <u>spiritual journeys</u> are always full of purpose and meaning. However, our journey requires that we step outside the line to reevaluate what we have been told by our conditioning and cultures. When we realize that we can step outside the line, we can then set a new course of direction. This will help us to define our purpose and focus, and allows us to accomplish the task. This simple step requires our input to the fullest of our ability for success to be accomplished.

Life's distractions often derail us from our goals and desires. But this only happens when we are <u>not</u> sure of our direction, or lack focus and belief in our purpose. This will make our errors or mistakes appear catastrophic, and will stop us in our tracks. This often halts or diminishes what we once believed to be a meaningful journey. So, if we are not sure of ourselves, we will not recognize that our mistakes are just an error——needing our correction.

Most often, we respond with the same old story, which is," This is how we have always done it!" And this is has never been very clear to us. These old methods are founded on judgment and confusion—— and not love or clarity! Yet, we continue to travel in that same old direction. It often takes many years before we find the courage to change our direction to find some joy and peace in our lives. We find ourselves living in the same old dreams of yesterday, wanting them to be true today. Our joy and happiness cannot be captured in our thoughts of yesterday. They are gone and can never return.

This is the process of the journey back, which is to allow us to continue to go forward and be happy! This directional change is natural, and is always about extensions— not projections.

To know the journey is to experience the moment, and to allow ourselves to take it in. Then we do not have to hold onto our dreams of yesterday as though they were today. This is what makes up "illusions". If we allow ourselves to get trapped there, then the clarity of our destination and purpose will become lost. Then, we find ourselves living in a constant dream— which has no real purpose or meaning.

How often have we had a friend tell us that they have been on their job for over twenty years, and hate what they do? But when you ask, "Why don't you leave?" they respond that they don't know, or that they need the money. Where is the clarity or the peace in that response? We must be willing to ask the question of ourselves— where we are going? It is important for us to open the door of awareness to ourselves, by recognizing that clarity can only be revealed when we seek it out, or we invite it in. This is the natural process of spirituality, which is to share love by extension, and this will always require our presence. We must be willing to step outside of the line of conformity so we may recognize ourselves and the loving being that we are.

Clarity is our key to the journey back and to making our spiritual connection. We must wake up and realize that <u>we are the source</u> of our joy, peace, and happiness. With the graces of God (our Creator), we can recognize that our journey is one of love and service! And by surrendering to the clear purpose of <u>love</u>, we will always find our way to peace.

When we look at our parents' motives they usually were made with good intentions. However, a lot of their messages were based on their own past experiences, which were just passed on through our lineage and belief system——but they were <u>not</u> based on truth. If we are to trust ourselves, we must come to recognize that <u>we are the source</u>, and to allow ourselves to become mindful. This will give us a natural connection to life itself! The simplicity of this mindful approach is acceptance, and it is always right there in front of us, to be recognized by those who choose to see it. Let the truth be told, that the <u>truth</u> can never be hidden. It can only be overlooked, or denied! To change something to fit our needs does not change the fact that it is still right there in front of us. This only tells us which of the two thought-systems we are using to choose our direction.

Destination

When we think of the term "journey," we can see many different destinations in our path. These range from taking a short trip across town, to that major trip to China. How do we discern which part of our life's journey is important and meaningful? And what does our final destination look like? I would like to think that all of the trips we have taken over the years have brought us closer to a clearer understanding of ourselves. If we can make this connection it will give us a closer relationship with our spiritual self— and to the Godliness that lies within.

The idea of a destination can be quite confusing when we are young. We often just live the dreams of our parents, rather than pursuing our own. This will make life quite confusing for some of us. How often have we seen a dad quite upset at his son's or daughter's baseball game? This could be over missing a ball, or in winning or losing of a game. Have you ever heard of two fathers wanting to "duke it out" in the parking lot to prove their point? Parents are great projectors of their emotions and dreams <u>to</u> their children. I remember a friend named Mary (who lived down the street) who hated the idea of becoming a professor like her mom and dad. She did everything in her power to be different from her parents. This created its own fight within her. She felt the need to keep this fight alive later in her life by not becoming a college graduate, even though she was very close to finishing a number of degrees.

Life's journey throws us a lot of different experiences at us, so we may continue to learn from them. However, it is important that we understand that not all experiences are supposed to be pleasurable for us. If we cannot accept this part the experience it will become quite unsettling for us, and will often lead to our fears. If this happens, we will generally run away from those experiences with a feeling of rejection or failure as a result. But often, in reality, the opposite is the case. All our experiences are there for our growth in one way or the other if we can only become mindful.

When we are able to be mindful, we will see the whole experience, and this will always leave us with a feeling of fullness and love. This feeling lets us recognize our growth and our blessings. How could a destination that brings such clarity ever be bad or harmful? For most of us, by the time we are in our late teens or early twenties, we start to understand that our destination is our own. And then, we can start to put forth the effort to claim it for ourselves.

Letting Go

This is where we must learn to look upon ourselves with different eyes. We must see ourselves as the loving and as spiritual being that we truly are. This is truly our destiny. As I stated earlier, every experience is there for our growth. We must learn to get out of our own way, so we may experience the moment for all it has to teach us.

This is not a process we are too familiar with, because we have usually been taught to be reactionary rather than being a receiver. It is hard to respond to something that we don't understand, or when we only have part of the story. Confusion is a large part of most stories, and our conditioning has governed most of our lives. This was the process or method we were taught by our parents and teachers who reinforced these concepts. Our societies have told us to be the best, and if we are <u>not</u> the best then we have failed. The emphasis was not placed on being the best person we can be. Society usually urged us to pursue and complete our goals, without any real regard to our spiritual being.

Love has but <u>one</u> direction, and seldom do we speak of this approach. The path of love tells us about our "Godliness," which is indeed a large part of us, and to acknowledge that one direction. To recognize this will allow us to see that a mistake is just an error needing correction. Most errors are but an experience that is without a clear or purposeful understanding. When we are connected to our spiritual self, all our actions become effortless and without waste—— and our path becomes clear. Then, each step we take appears to be smooth, and without effort.

What Is Our Purpose?

The dictionary tells us that a purpose is the reason for something to exist, or the reason it was done, or to have a intended or desired result. Perhaps we need to understand our purpose from our spiritual point of view, and to understanding that most of us do <u>not</u> see ourselves from this point of view. Without a clear purpose we can easily get lost and confused–thus making our journey meaningless. The journey that is without service to the whole would be like having a purpose without meaning.

When we look around us, we see a lot of activity in our everyday lives, but there is little or no <u>service</u> being shared. We look at the wasteful approach of our government and the governments around the world. They demonstrate how little service is being rendered. Our purpose must begin with the love of self, and with that purposeful understanding we have united with our brothers in the oneness we share. We will recognize that they are our teachers, and we are theirs. However, to feel this purpose, we must see the <u>union</u> of our existence, and not the separation. The union tells us that we are the same, and in that sameness there is no difference. Yet, our eyes will show us the differences of our bodies, which confuses us to our clear purpose. When we love ourselves, we will be able to see beyond the body and our mistakes–to recognize our oneness and purpose, which is to love.

Our conditioning tells us that we are different, and yet in our spirits we cannot stand alone. But most often those things that we don't understand, we are afraid of–and tell ourselves they should not be trusted. When there is no union between us, we can only focus on our differences, and this will create mistrust and attacks. We have been conditioned to doubt, and to walk with fear. This conditioning does not allow us to come to grips with the journey back, because it commands us to stay in line. *We* must learn to see ourselves with this light of love that dwells in our hearts! Then, we will recognize this was our gift from birth–knowing that we are all connected.

This connection will lead us back to the idea of our oneness, which is more about us and our union rather than our separation. This is the process of WIN -WIN. Most of us see our goals and our purpose as something we have to accomplish. However, when we have met those goals, they are often not what we thought they should be and there is always something empty about our accomplishments.

Let me tell you a story about a man who had climbed to the top of his company and was very successful. He believed this would make him happy. He lived in a nice house, in a nice part of town, with a loving family. He always purchased the nicest of things, and he thought this is what success was all about. He also always had a fantasy about a particular car that costs some $138,000.00. There were only a few of these cars made every year, making them very special.

The day came when he was to pick up his new car, and he asked his old friend to come along. He had told his friend many times over the years how much he wanted this car. As they drove off the lot of the dealership, his buddy looked at him and asked what was wrong. His facial expression was not that of joy or excitement, but one of disappointment and unhappiness. He looked at his friend and shockingly said, "I feel lousy." The friend asked why, since you wanted this car for so long, and now you have it, what could be wrong? He acknowledge that his friend was right, but added that his satisfaction was <u>not</u> what he thought it would be. He went on to explain that he thought this would make him feel happy, and give him some type of fulfillment. But, later, he realized that he felt nothing from this accomplishment——it was just a car! He realized that he had lost sight of his goal, which was not about an object, but was about love and union instead.

Most of us will put our hopes in those things that we believe have value and will make us happy. Later, we realize that these things give us little or nothing in return that is lasting. To acquire an object is just an acquisition! An object has no feeling of its own and cannot give anything in return. That has never been the function of any object. If our purpose "lacks clarity", then how can we have joy or happiness as an outcome? How can we have this joy or happiness if we have not made a connection to our spiritual self? We must understand that the service of our oneness comes from within. Our true <u>purpose</u> is always about the whole, and not about Me or Mine. We are not alone, and have never been alone. The journey back has always been about <u>our</u> union and wholeness. Being able to recognize our connection to our spiritual self is about the love of <u>self</u>, and that we must learn to share.

The thought-system we use to accomplish any goal must come from within us. This is why we find ourselves confused in our search for love and happiness, because we lose sight of where it comes from. We choose to search for them <u>outside</u> of the <u>source</u>, in a place where they can never be found. We find ourselves riding on this roller coaster of life, which never seems to end. But this is the thought-system we have chosen to use (driven by our ego), and it is always based on fear. And our ego has no real understanding of love or happiness attached to it, because its actions are based on either fear or confusion.

Actions that are driven by our egos will never have a clear purpose, they only allow us to be reactionary. Even after we have accomplished our goals, there is little (if any) internal fulfillment that comes with our results. We find ourselves living out the journey of our society, which is not always concerned with the idea of love or peace.

We need to ask if we really want love and happiness in our lives. To answer that question, we must look at the things necessary to have love and happiness in the first place. Love and happiness are not so elusive when we understand where they come from (the source). Then, we realize that they are not hidden from us at all. They are with us every day; but we are not able to see them because we deny their presence. This denial happens because of our own confusion and conditioning, which is driven by the fear of the unknown. Marianne Williamson in her book, A Return to Love states that, "Our deepest fear is not that we are inadequate. Our deepest fear is that we are powerful beyond measure."

Most of our decisions are fear based. This is not because we want to be afraid; it's because we are not conscious of our confusion. So, if we cannot see the clarity of our actions, how can we have an understanding of what actions should be taken?

The Need To Love Ourselves

Every one of us wants love. It is a natural feeling, because it is the gift to all of us from God (our Creator). This makes it natural to love as a part of our being. However, we have often denied the presence of our "Godliness," and our love! But, with this denial, we can only live out the life we thought it should be, and never make the connection with the love it is.

However, for us to make this connection, we must recognize that we are confused. This will allow us to see how we have gone wrong and without a true understanding of love. Confusion is but an illusion of our own projections and desires, and <u>not</u> a part of truth at all.

Some people find it hard to truly love, because most of us function with the energy of our egos—— which is about separation. This ego-energy looks upon everything with contempt and comparison, and creates doubt. This will always have us ambivalent in our responses. With this suspicious and confused attitude, we will never be able to experience true love or peace. This is the attitude or thought-system of our egos, which wants us to believe that misery and suffering are the end-product of our journey. However, by accepting our hardship as a transitional process, we can have self-love.

Hardships or "set-backs" are just a temporary phase in our lives. We must see these phases as a transitional process that will pass on, so we may focus on the new light, rather than on our immediate problem. This <u>new</u> <u>light</u> (or source) comes from our inner-godliness. It helps us make the connection, so we may overcome our setback with love, and with an "enlightened" direction.

Until we let go of the <u>wrong</u> teachers (our ego), we will continue to follow the wrong message. This will not allow us to experience the loving-being that is within us. So, we must surrender to the knowing that we are all whole— and full of love to make our connection.

Our ego is terrified of this part of us making this connection because it would lose all of its control if we recognize our wholeness. It does not want us to recognize this love within us. So, it hides true love from us, and gives us the illusions of love, instead. By doing this, our ego never allows us to see the substitutions we make to represent love. These desires and projections become our substitutions to what we believe is real. They also make us deny that part of us that is loving. We need to stop looking at ourselves with comparison and ambivalence, for this always fosters confusion.

To make these changes, we must be willing to go inside (where there is no confusion or ambivalence), where our direction is clear and unobstructed. Love and peace have only <u>one direction</u>, and can only reflect themselves. This choice must always be made of free will. Our Creator will never attack our choice, even when our direction is not in accord with this source. True love always travels with the companion of patience (which is our Creator's gift), helping us to recognize and understand what we truly want. We cannot tell ourselves that we want to change and then do nothing to bring it about. This is but the illusion of our ego giving us false directions. We need to realize that this is not a logical mode of action.

Love is like a good investment— it is always simple! If we take our time and let it unfold before us, then the experience can become wonderful. That is not about the good or bad, it is just the facts! That is the gift of love. It is important that we understand that we block the light of our love by trying to alter it. However, when we surrender to the choice of love (consciously or unconsciously), we open that door to our Creator's love, which is always right in front of us. Then, we will no longer need the <u>idea</u> <u>of</u> <u>love</u> to fill our lives, because wholeness and oneness are one in the same.

The understanding of wholeness is merely to understand universal laws—that connect us all. This is needed for us to let go of the duality and separation that we have so long embraced, and which has keep us from being loving.

This is necessary as an acknowledgement to recognize our Creator, which is inside of us, so we may be aware of our blessing. Then, the love we <u>seek</u> will appear as though it were a miracle! To have this clear understanding <u>is</u> a miracle, because clearly a miracle is being presented! It is only in our bewilderment of an event, that we make it unclear, and thus confusing. These conflicting thoughts keep us confused about ourselves and about our love. We must open our hearts, for our Creator's love to come in, and this can only happen by our invitation!

Erasing The Confusion And Fear

The universal laws that are set in motion will always create a particular outcomes and will require that we obey these laws.

Whatever direction we have chosen must adhere to these laws. Our choices are not about coercion of any kind, because coercion cannot be about love. Free-will is imperative in our choice to give love; it is always about giving, not taking. What is eternal can only come from the whole—— and the spirit is whole! This was a gift that I heard about from Nelson Mandela, as he was being interviewed some years back. He spoke of his prison guards with such love and humility even though he was in prison. This spoke to me very deeply as to what true love must really mean. It allowed me to recognize that true love comes from inside of us as an eternal gift of life. This supported the universal laws, given by our Creator as our birthright!

Most of our goals and accomplishments have not been clear, because they did not reflect the union of our oneness, or love. We find ourselves focusing on being right, or in control and looking for our own gain. This approach can be quite confusing. We find ourselves fixated on the objects or the goals themselves, and not on the process that takes us there. This often means we cannot share the experiences with others, because we lack in the understanding of the process. This also means that it is possible for us to get hurt along the way, when we do not understand the process.

This happens when we have lost sight of the service to the whole. We believe we are alone, and this aloneness breeds mistrust and fear. But, we are never alone, and need to recognize this to feel our "oneness in spirit." This will allow us to feel our spiritual connection and erase our fears. This connection will give us the strength to make the journey back.

To make goals is not a bad thing. However, the way we were taught to approach them lacks the understanding of our union. We were taught <u>not</u> to look at the process, but to bring about results or a finished project. Let's assume that two men were traveling to the same destination. One man was told to climb a hilly mountainside; while the other man travels a route of flat terrain. The destination of their journey was to be the same, but our conditioning will tell us that one is better than the other due to the terrain. When we look at it from another point of view, both men must start by taking the first step. However, usually our poor perception of the situation traps us, letting us see only our problems, rather than appreciating it as an opportunity to grow.

Once we have let go of our misperceptions of tomorrow, then <u>all</u> possibilities will be seen as part of the journey. Misperception never allows us to feel connected to the journey. It keeps us from recognizing that we are in our own way. It is rare for us to accept the situation as it is, because this is not the way we were taught to approach our lives. When we take a close look at what we control about our tomorrow, we come to realize it is very little. The acknowledgment of this fact could give us comfort if we merely accepted it as a part of our journey.

I have often thought I was in control, but once I started to take a situation or circumstance apart, I realized, I was just a participant in the process ----and not in control at all! The more I became at peace with that fact, the less I stressed over tomorrow. At that point, I was just surrendering to the feeling of oneness, and to the presence of my spiritual-self. However, it is important to realize that we need to surrender to the process-------and God (our Creator) will do the rest!

This is so hard for some of us, because we have been told all of our lives to take control, to be in charge, and to make things happen. To sit back (and go with the flow) is truly foreign to most of us. So, we fight this approach with a great deal of vigor.

How can we ever love ourselves if we are in a constant state of conflict with ourselves?

Most of us will admit that we have some type of fear as a major part of our lives, even when we cannot identify what we are afraid of. So, when looking at how to identify our fears, we must look at the thought-system we use to govern our lives. We must understand that every thought is driven by a particular action helping us to define who we think we are— and the belief-system that it supports.

There are only two thought-systems we use to define ourselves: one being that of Love and Peace, the other of fear and confusion. This is why it is of critical importance to recognize, and to become aware of, which thought-system we are using to determine our actions.

When looking at a definition of fear, it could be seen as a series of emotions of one's own confusion (not being understood), and thus turning these emotions against oneself, creating internal conflict.

The recognition of the thought-system we use is a critical part in processing our fears. To change directions, we must understand where we are now. This requires us to be mindful of our choices, and the particular thought-system we use to make them. Thus, bringing together clarity and understanding, and not fear or confusion to our direction. However, most of us move with such an automatic response, we do not think about a mindful approach very much at all. This could only lead to more confusion, because if we do not understand what we are doing, and why we are doing it, then how could anyone else? This leads us to believe that <u>both</u> thought-systems are inter-changeable.

Allowing us to believe that <u>truth</u> and <u>illusion</u> can go together. This could never be true! The Truth cannot be altered and still remain the Truth. So, we must recognize that illusions are but a fantasy of our desires——a projection that carries no power of Truth at all. Yet, we hold on to them with great expectations. This keeps us confused and fearful. It is imperative that we understand that to hold on to our concealment of our fears and desires has harmed our spirit and our connection. It has created a split-mind as to who we are. We need another way of looking at ourselves; a mindful approach of seeing our love, without confusion or fear.

Looking At Fear

Fear always comes with the <u>absence</u> of faith. *Fear is but a poor understanding of what is there. This causes us to fear our own misperceptions, and creates a never ending conflict within.*

Faith is about receiving the union of any experience. By surrendering to that experience, we are able to accept the glory and the blessing of that moment. Faith is <u>beyond</u> belief, and must be experienced to be understood.

However, <u>faithlessness</u> dwells in darkness, and looks upon everything with doubt, never letting us see clearly what is there. It clouds our decision on what we see, and this makes it hard to make the right choice. Here lies the thought-system of our ego, and the energy it would have us think with. The ego wants us to walk with fear as our companion, and to use judgment and doubt as our means to process. Fear and faith can never be companions by the <u>nature</u> of how they function. Fear always travels with concealment, and with this a need to hide. This leads us to separation and to be mistrustful.

Fear will always have us search for the answers in the wrong place. It traps us in the past, or lets us project into the future, and neither of these choices are based on reality. This is the criteria set forth by our ego's thought-system, which is fear and confusion.

Faith (on the other hand) is but a reflection of <u>truth</u> and <u>love</u>, and it needs our <u>presence</u> to be recognized and understood. Faith removes all limitations, and allows us to witness the whole. Where there is Truth, illusion cannot be! Truth can only reflect what is in front of us—— and this is never fearful.

Denial Of Truth

Denials <u>can</u> and <u>do</u> create their own differences. When we try to change what is already there, we choose to deny Truth. We then go on to tell ourselves that we understand the reality of a particular situation, when actually we are terrified. How could this bring on anything other than confusion and fear? This loop of fear and confusion is but a form of conditioning that we have bought into.

To deny is to change that which is <u>natural,</u> and to make it into something that is different or <u>unnatural</u>. This is a process of wanting to undo what has already been done. Our beliefs are based on our fixed perception that gives us the foundation of who we believe we are. To remember God (our Creator) is very natural for some of us, but, for others, this denial becomes their truth. Then, we must create a belief-system or definitions which allow us to believe something different. But, confused by what we have created, we now question the foundation of our own beliefs.

Not understanding our own creation has left us feeling neurotic and fearful. With these feelings we realize that our creation cannot be shared. Then, we must now question the foundation of our own beliefs. We must now look at the darkness and light, and recognize that they can not both occupy the same space. But, whatever we have told ourselves, is real, we now believe this is our truth and have accepted it as our reality.

This also means that we cannot see the pure light within ourselves, because we have chosen to alter what is there. Remember, we do not <u>create</u> truth, it is merely <u>revealed</u> to us. To accept the dilemma of our own creation will create barriers and walls of differences between us. This will have us maintain, and hold onto, a level of separation, which we have created. This will put a stranglehold on the <u>universal</u> belief-system that we are all one in union.

Our parents usually were not taught to be mindful of this truth. They were conditioned in the same way we were, just in a different time. Our denials make us focus on those small things that show us that we're different, and here lies the catch—— they are often founded on illusions! These small parts would <u>not</u> even be recognizable if we did not focus so hard on them. Accepting the ego as our ally, we then accept confusion as our fundamental criteria, thus making this <u>tiny</u> part enormous. For example, like telling your partner that you are going to be for them when in your heart you know you can not. Yet you allow yourself to live out the lie to keep face.

Could our Creator reverse our thinking on this subject? Perhaps, but this would not be of our free-will. We were created <u>free,</u> and without limits, to be able to reflect our <u>likeness</u> to God (our Creator) in spirit not in body. However, God (our Creator) needs to be invited into our hearts, so we may reflect our likeness and free-will.

This recognition will give us faith (and the ability to heal) through clarity and understanding. It is a sign that we have accepted the love of God (our Creator). This reflection can only be shared by the whole, in which we all are a part of.

Faith is an acknowledgment of this oneness and union. It is the profound acknowledgment (to every one of us) that peace and love are a natural part of our lives. This was given to us as our natural inheritance. The whole must (by its nature) reflect all parts. When we learn to walk with <u>love</u> and <u>faith,</u> we will no longer look upon our brother or sister with faithlessness. We will no longer tell ourselves that they are unworthy of our love. Faith guides our vision so we are able to see ourselves, and recognize that we are already free—— and that is the nature of the whole!

Need For Acceptance

Acceptance is a prerequisite for <u>faith;</u> we can not have one without the other. Accepting requires that we surrender a part of ourselves to an understanding of something far greater than our knowing. This allows us to understand that our <u>knowing</u> is greater than our intellectual basis. Here is where faith removes <u>all</u> limitations, and allows us to get out of our way—— so the truth may be revealed! However, we must be patient, and have a <u>willingness</u> to surrender. Acceptance is not about the outcome that we would like to happen; it is about the one that has already happened. In understanding this approach, we are no longer trapped by the illusions, fantasies, or the need to be right. If we believe that we know the right way, we have already made a <u>projection</u>, and we are living in the future, at that point. We must remember that we do not create Truth ——we are only the observer of it! Yes, indeed, we <u>do</u> participate in the event, but we do not create its outcome.

Acceptance allows us to see the Truth (absent of the illusions), by allowing us to realize that we are only part of the whole. We must see the <u>whole</u> to understand our small part. This is to recognize what "whole" means, and to see our participation in what we see as the whole. The ego would have us believe that illusion can reflect both truth and whole. But illusions reflect the past (which is gone and will never return), or create projections into tomorrow (which is not real, because it has not yet arrived). Truth can only reflect itself, right now, and nothing more. We can not create the "now"; we can only experience it, in our observation. This is why it is imperative for us to surrender to the process of acceptance.

Acceptance allow us to not be afraid of the outcome, regardless of what it may reveal. This means that we are willing to accept the Truth without alteration. The moment we start to alter the truth, it is no longer <u>universal</u> Truth. The greater the depth of our mindfulness, the more we will understand our inter-connectedness.

This is to say that we are participants in the actions and the outcome we see, but we do not create them. Even though we have the right to choose our directions, most of us are <u>not</u> conscious enough to make wise or sound choices. We often make our choices based on our conditioning and common patterns of our belief-system——which we created, and have accepted as our Truth. However, do these images reflect truth, or merely our conditioned-behavior?

Mindfulness

Being mindful is about looking at ourselves in every possible way. It allows us to look at ourselves without judgment of what we see. This gives us a chance to see the <u>whole</u> picture, and not just the small part that we deemed as whole. We look at our behavioral pattern and conditioning to see what is there. This gives us a chance to take in the situation, because we are no longer looking for a particular outcome. To be mindful means to allow ourselves the joy of experiencing the moment, unedited by our actions. When we are aware, it requires no solicited action by us, at all. It merely requires our presence for it to be enjoyed.

Being mindful could also represent a form of meditation. It can help us to center ourselves through our breath. Meditation has been known to help in calming our stress and to help with focusing our concentration. It has long been proven that learning how to focus on <u>our breath</u> is very beneficial to our health and well-being. It helps us to connect with our spirit. This is not a method that requires a lot of effort on our part, because we use our breath all the time. However, we are not very mindful of this process of breathing. I will speak more on the benefits of meditation in later chapters.

We need to recognize that every event is unfolding right before our eyes. But, it is imperative that we do <u>not</u> try to tell ourselves that we know the outcome—— before it happens. If we get ahead of ourselves, we will become trapped in the idea that we know the outcome—— before it is revealed! This could only lead us to manifest an outcome of our choosing, and to deny the one that was revealed. Mindfulness ask that we allow <u>acceptance</u> to be our ally, in our journey back to understanding how to love.

Meditation is another means to help us sort out the confusion of facts from fiction. It allows us to not be trapped by the images of our imagination. They will confuse us when it comes to our true iden-tity. The belief that we can create or choose a particular outcome is only the denial of acceptance. This denial goes against the natural laws of the universe, and these laws never need our input—only our acceptance!

Natural laws (by their nature) would have us learn to walk with balance in all our relationships, and with all things. Then we can recognize our one-mindedness, with God our Creator. The most interesting part about choosing our own way is that we don't know what it is we want in the first place! For example, look at all the times that we have made a choice to do something or go to a particular event. Later we realize that we were not happy with our choice. When we made a purchase of a new suit and before we got home we decided to return it, or to make a career change, and shortly after our decision, we are displeased with our choice. The point here is that we are often confused by our own deci-sions. Acceptance only asks that we surrender to the spiritual part of us—this part we have so long denied. It brings about a clarity and peace to your decision, because it reflects the whole picture.

Our spiritual connection is a natural part of us, and we must become mindful of its presence. Mindfulness can only reflect the images that are in front of us, and this is all that is real. This means we would have to let go of the idea of controlling the moment, and this is very fearful for most of us.

But the truth of the matter is that we are <u>out</u> <u>of</u> <u>control</u> most of the time, and don't even recognize this fact. We like to tell ourselves that we have everything under control. This is how the ego disguises what it wants us to see to make it what we <u>want</u>, later to recognize that it is not real.

Faith is much like being mindful, it only acknowledges the things that are there. This truth leads to the fact that the whole must reflect all parts. When we learn to walk with <u>love</u> in our hearts, we will no longer judge our brothers, but love them instead. Love them for what they are, and not for who we want them to be. Then, faith will remove all limitations, so we may see the whole.

Meditation has proven to be a great technique in helping us make our connection. By learning how to meditate, we start to become mindful, as a by-product of meditation. When using a mindful approach to touch our center (spirit), the journey becomes easier. We already know how to breathe, so we do not need to learn something new. We merely need to learn how to focus on our breath. The breath is already a part of us, and for that reason it will not take long for us to see the results. No one person or culture holds the key to helping us touch our spiritual self, because this journey is about self-discovery. As we look at this approach of breathing we understand that it does not differentiate among Buddhists, Christians, Hindus, Sikhs, Jews or Muslims. Nor does it see the differences of class, or whether we are rich or poor, conservative or liberals. If we can learn to focus on the breath, it will bring a mindful understanding of <u>who</u> <u>we</u> <u>are</u> at a level we have <u>not</u> yet explored. Allowing ourselves to recognize our breath as an <u>extension</u> of us, will lead us to a place of <u>compassion</u> for ourselves and others.

When we look at the idea of a journey back, it stands to reason that it would cross our mind to ask from where are we journeying back from? To do this, we need to look at our spiritual journey: and to ask where <u>we</u> <u>have</u> <u>been</u> (to know where), <u>we</u> <u>are</u> <u>going</u>. This is to reference the idea that we have lost a part of something. This is to remember what it means, to say that (we had to have it), in order to lose it. This speaks to the title of this book, <u>Have We Lost Our Spiritual Connection</u>?

Certainty and Clarity have always been there as a part of the universal laws, put there to govern the universe. These laws have no contradictions to them, and we all function under these universal laws. Therefore, if a contradiction occurred, it would have to be due to <u>man-law</u>, rather than <u>universal</u> <u>law</u>. The problem here is that when we follow <u>man-laws</u>, they (in many instances) are not <u>just</u> or universal. They will never allow us to live with certainty—— only doubt and fear.

As we discovered the idea of free-will, we realized that it came with the ability to choose. However, there has never been a clear understanding as to why these choices came with uncertainty and doubt. Perhaps it is because they were derived from confusion. For the most part, we were never told to become mindful, or to understand our direction. We were just told to pursue the goals of "getting a big house" or getting a "nice job" or to have fame or stardom.

When we see the universe in such a fragmented form, we can no longer see it as whole. Then only doubt and fear will become our focus. We will not be able hear our inner-voice, and this will create our denial. We have taken the universal laws, and made them man-Laws. Taking what is natural and making it be unnatural creates separation and difference. We've lost ourselves in what is not there.

However, if we choose to use our free will to go against the universal laws, it will create unbalanced approach. This will lead to our misperception of the events we encounter, and give us the belief that they are the norm. Then we will label these misperceptions as symbolic with meaning that only a few know or understand. This produces multiplicity: giving us many things from which to choose, and creating much confusion. The divine laws given to us were not about authority or power. These laws were given to us to bring forth balance and justice. We need to make these divine laws our beacon to the light of oneness, and to our journey back.

CHAPTER 6
Miracles of Mindfulness

Miracles are a surprising and welcomed event that are not explainable by natural or scientific laws—and they are considered to be divine. Miracles are a subject that is fascinating to most of us, and yet quite perplexing at the same time. Miracles are that moment in time that we cannot explain. They are that moment which releases what just happened. The nature of a miracle is beyond our understanding. This is because we have forgotten that clarity and understanding is what makes up a miracle. We have taught ourselves <u>not</u> to identify with anything other than our bodies. Miracles go far beyond our body. But we need to remember our essence (spiritual connection) to recognize that fact, and that we are far more than just our bodies.

When we no longer see the limits in ourselves (and in our brothers), we will start to recognize the oneness that we all share. And here lies the miracle. The gift of God (our Creator) removes our limits, so we may see the whole——that oneness that we all share!

If we allow ourselves to think about the limitations of the next few seconds clearly, we will realize that we are not truly conscious of these few seconds. We merely accept the outcome of those few seconds, and then alter them to fit our definition of what we believed we just experienced. We are not really capable of explaining what just happened. However, our belief-system takes over, and we merely accept our old patterns. Here in lies the complexity in miracles.

Science has told us that miracles are of some supernatural power, and that we do not possess this power. Religion has said that miracles are of a Divine Intervention, and again makes us believe that this power is <u>beyond</u> us. We need to ask ourselves: "If another persona is capable of performing a miracle, then could we also believe that this power is within us, as well?" The answer to this question lies in us asking if we have stopped to look at it in a mindful way and to look at our clarity.

Yes, we are Godly, and perform miracles all the time. We just need to be reminded of this fact. Mindfulness is the choice of assessment and awareness questioning who we are, <u>beyond</u> the body. By looking beyond our body, we recognizes we are connected to the universe, and realize it is complete and whole—just like we are!

When we can escape the fear of wanting to know our true-self, we will discover love, and the union within us. This is not what the body shows us on a daily basis. It wants us to look upon our brother and sister with contempt. We must understand that bodies can never join, only <u>minds</u> can! We need to understand that our bodies can only take the directions given by our minds.

Mindfulness

QUESTION: When we were kids, and did something wrong or something we shouldn't have, how did our moms always seem to know?

This implies an intuitive part of our mom's that give them that wholeness. That oneness which allows our parents to be connected to us, and to know when something is wrong. Another example of this would be when we are talking with our dad over the phone (from thousands of miles away), and he was often able to discern (by our tone of voice) that something was wrong. Again, how can this be?

When <u>love</u> is present, there is also a connection of minds. This is God's (our Creator's) gift to us. And the circumstances do not have to be family or even friendship related, to make them a mindful connection. The only thing required is that we must have love in our <u>hearts</u>, and not be afraid to share this connection.

Mindfulness only asks that we "let it be what it is." We must allow ourselves to merely examine the event and not try to change it. The growth and change will come automatically. Nothing is required, but to have <u>acceptance</u> of the moment or experience. This is where miracles reside in the process of acceptance. Whether they are large or small, difficult or easy, long or short, it does not matter to the clarity or understanding of a miracle. It is beyond the understanding of our physical self, or the rules and laws made by mankind.

We are not told to be <u>mindful</u>, but rather told to follow the rules passed on by our scholars and forefathers. Mindfulness requires us to step outside the boundaries of education and conditioning, to see what is truly right in front of us. This truth is always there, but it is <u>not</u> always seen. This could be due to the influence of the ego. The ego has a major fear of its own in not wanting us to understand our mindful approach. The ego recognizes that if we become mindful, it loses its hold on our being. This means the ego needs to keep conflict present, in order to continue to direct our lives with fear and confusion.

Mindfulness requires an assessment, which can often lead to acceptance. Our belief-systems are very powerful in our lives. We have been taught to change or alter the things we see to make them fit or work for us. The question we need to ask in making these changes is "have we ever achieved the perfect plan?" Usually, the answer is "no." Most often the outcome of our best plan, never completely pleased us. If we are not pleased, there could not have been an accurate assessment or acceptance of our plan. And yet, there is always growth in grasping for perfection. Growth comes from our best effort, and nothing more is needed!

To believe that something is possible, we have to "get out of our way" of what we believe it can be. We must be willing to let go of many of the things we have been taught to believe in and to what is possible. We need to allow ourselves to asses our discovery, then something wonderful will take place! This is what mindfulness will do for us; it defines the holy instant and gives it meaning. This is why an assessment is required.

When we look at being mindful, we are generally searching for clarity and understanding of what just happened. Our spirit wants us to be mindful, and to surrender to the holy instant. Searching with equal effort for our attention is our ego which uses its clever method to keep us confused about what it is we see. It wants us to alter what we see to fit the outcome we would like to see. Yet, the interesting thing about this approach is that we can never seem to get the outcome we want—we can only get close.

The ego's approach never gives us a clear answer. It just continues to have us create more questions. If our answers are never certain, we will always be with doubt about ourselves and our brothers. Even when we have felt that we are correct, there is still that question of doubt or uncertainty about our direction.

This is the cleverness of our ego: it keep us searching for the phantom answer, the one with no real conclusion. It never allows us to experience love or peace. It only wants us to see the illusion of these experiences as they appear before our eyes. The ego has no true understanding of Truth or Love. It can only bring the idea of these thoughts to our mind, and then have us develop them to our liking (on its behalf). Remember, Truth is not created by us— merely revealed to us.

QUESTION: If the Truth could be so easily altered, would it still be the truth?

Or would this create a continuum of confusion and doubt about the truth? In assessing the truth I have often realized that it was always there. It was not created; it was just there—to be accepted or denied. This is one of the two thought-systems we choose to use in making our decisions.

Science On Miracles

The typical misconception about science is that it can tell us what has happened in the past or is going to happen in the future (given enough time). But the fact of the matter is that science can only give us a limited understanding of what took place. It does not deal with the ideas of absolute truth, but only to a degree of probability. Science observes the universe, records its evidence, and strives to draw rational conclusions about its findings. It is concerned with what happened in the past, or to look at the potential outcomes of the future. But, neither of these deals with the idea of absolute Truth, or the idea of God (our Creator).

Science does not tell us what will <u>always</u> be with any level of certainty. However, it does tell us what has already been observed or what will most certainly be observed in the future. So, when enough evidence is gathered and all that evidence points to the same truth, this yields to an extremely high level of fact, then science is often labeled as the truth.

The probability of the same truth always existing is considered to be beyond doubt, and from this truth we make "man-laws." Therefore, the laws of science are highly respected and considered to be essentially beyond doubt. However, because these laws are made by mankind, there is always the slightest potential that a law could be broken in the future by some unknown event. This makes "probability" the cornerstone of science. Mark Kac, a famous Polish mathematician and professor at Cornell and Rockefeller Universities, said, "Probability is a cornerstone of all the sciences, and its daughter, the science of statistics." This enters into all human activities (as quoted in Smith,1975, p.111, emp.added)

Universal Laws

The law of Cause and Effect states that every material effect must have an adequate antecedent or simultaneous cause. Causality (also referred to as causation) is the relationship between events the first cause, and a second is the effect, where the second event is understood as a consequence of the first. Like the energy of the Tsunami of 2004 in Malaysia and Thailand, there must be an adequate cause for a tidal wave of this magnitude, and it is likely to be found in an underwater earthquake. Another simpler example of this is when we throw a ball into a glass window, and seeing the glass shatter as a result. The ball hitting the glass being the <u>effect,</u> and our actions the catalyst for the contact, or cause.

The idea of cause and effect is based on the processing of any given experience, and the result or definition that follows making it what it is. Here lies the confusion. If we believe that we are the source of our <u>truth</u>, and that our reality is a reflection of that moment. We will then tell ourselves that we are the creator of this reality. If we tell ourselves that we are the source (Creator), then wouldn't we know or have the knowledge of the cause? But in many cases this is only due to a frequent use of particular patterns, which have allowed us to make the repetitions of our habits, and calling it the source. This could also be a form of our conditioning. This conditioning has led us to accept things (because of what we have seen or experienced), and then made them into our reality. However, this is really just a poor understanding of the source, by us accepting the condition or customs as the source. If matter were not created, and put in our universe, we would not exist as we do today. Can we tell ourselves we understand this, or have we just accepted the patterns as they are? The miracle part of this is what we are supposed to discover. But, if we did not create universal-laws, then the question where did they come from?

This speaks to another law termed "Thermodynamic," which comes from a two rooted word: Thermo (meaning heat) and dynamic (meaning power). Thus, the laws of thermodynamics are the laws of "Heat Power." As far as we can tell, these laws are absolute. All things in the observable universe are affected by, and obey these laws of thermodynamics. The First law of Thermodynamics is commonly known as the _law of Conservation_ of matter. This law states that matter and energy cannot be <u>created</u>, nor can they be <u>destroyed</u>, and that the quantity of matter and energy must remain the same. It can change forms (from solid to gas to plasma and back again), but the total amount of matter and energy in the universe remains constant.

Here, again, we have a bit of science and miracle mixed together. This is the first law of thermodynamics; and these laws mankind did <u>not</u> create. However, we are to observe and become aware of how to use such complex laws of the universe. Could this be a miracle, or a gift from God (our Creator), since the law is universal?

Historically, thermodynamics developed out of a desire to increase the efficiency of early steam engines, particularly through the work of French physicist Nicolas Leonard Sadi Carnot (1824), who believed that the efficiency of heat-engines was the key that could help France win the Napoleonic Wars. Sadi Carnot, the French engineer interested in designing an efficient steam engine, is considered the founder of thermodynamics.

In 1824, he published "Reflection on the motive Power of Fire". In this article, he founded the Carnot's principle, or what we call today the Second Law of thermodynamics. Carnot showed the work produced by a steam engine is proportional to the heat transferred from the boiler to the condenser, and work could only be gained (from heat) by a transfer from a warmer to a colder body. The principle was never applied during Carnot's lifetime; he died of cholera, at the age of 36. Rudolf Clausius restated Carnot's principle as: the work produced by heat is not only proportional to the heat transferred from the warmer to the colder body, but is also proportional to the temperature difference of the two bodies. Clausius formulated the **second law,** and coined the term "entropy" after the Greek word meaning transformation. According to Clasius, "entropy" was the amount of thermal energy not available to do work, or the opposite of energy.

The first thermodynamic textbook was written in 1859 by William Rankine. Originally trained as a physicist and a civil and mechanical engineer, he was a professor at the University of Glasgow. The first and second laws of thermodynamics emerged simultaneously (in the 1850's), primarily from the works of William

Rankine, Rudolf Clausius, and William Thomson 1st Baron (Lord Kelvin).

The Second Law of Thermodynamics states that, "in all energy exchanges, if no energy enters or leaves the system, the potential energy of the state will always be less than that of the initial state." This also is commonly referred to as **Entropy.** This is like a car that has run out of gas and will need to be refueled for its energy source. A tank of gasoline has a certain potential energy that is converted into kinetic energy by the engine. Energy is defined as the ability to do work. Like the cells in our body, and how they convert potential energy, (usually in the form of C-C covalent bonds or ATP molecules), into kinetic energy to accomplish cell division, growth, biosynthesis and active transport, among other things.

We can also look at entropy as lost energy, which can bring on depression as a condition of low energy. This is all designed to be in a closed system, which the universe is.

These laws are finely tuned in their design, and they are applied to the whole universe, without exception. This would make these laws appear as miracles, wouldn't you say?

Miracles at this level can only be performed by our Creator or God. How can we have such a <u>creation</u>, without a <u>creator</u>? Science performs miracles all the time, by its understanding of the working of our heart, brains, and circulatory system, just to name a few. This knowledge and understanding has sent man to the moon, and created computers. How can we <u>not</u> see these acts performed by man as miracles? This is why the universal laws are there, and helping us to realize what is possible.

How could we <u>not</u> have this kind of clarity, when Jesus Christ has stated that we share these qualities with our creator? The message here is for us to understand what a miracle is, and to let <u>us</u> know that <u>we</u> have these powers, as well. This would mean that we must also "be Godly," and part of the universal law.

Religion And Miracles

In many circles, miracles often denote an event attributed to by divine intervention. Some others have suggested that God (our Creator) may work with the laws of nature to perform what we perceive as miracles. Others believe that a miracle is a phenomenon; not fully explainable or known by the laws of man. Some others will say these acts come by some supernatural entity, or by some unknown or outside force.

Religion can be seen as a collection of cultural systems, and a belief system that relates to our humanity and spirituality. Most of the beliefs or concerns in religion are focused on the cause and the nature of the universe. It especially wants us to consider our moral values. This involves devotional and ritual observances, and often contains a moral code governing the conduct of human affairs. It is seen as a specific fundamental set of beliefs and practices generally agreed upon by a number of persons or sect, much like the Christian religion or the Buddhist religion.

Many religions have narratives, symbols, traditions and sacred histories that are intended to give meaning to life or to explain the origin of life or the universe.

The word "religion" is sometimes used interchangeably with faith or belief systems, but religion differs from most private belief systems in that it has a public aspect.

The practice of most religions may also include sermons, commemoration of the activities of a god or gods, sacrifices, festivals, feasts, trance, initiations, meditation, public service or other aspects of human culture.

The development of religion has taken different forms in different cultures. Most religions place an emphasis on belief, while others emphasize practice. Some religions focus on the subjective experience of the religious individual. While others consider the activities of the religious community, or to create a relationship to be the most important. Some religions claim to be universal, and believe their laws and cosmology to be binding for everyone. While others are intended to be practiced only by a closely defined or localized group.

I believe that all religions are reaching for the same thing; the goal of having us touch that spiritual part of ourselves. In hope that this will allow us to make a connection with our spirit, which is acquired through faith, and necessary to find peace. This faith cannot be defined by a word. Faith speaks to the belief that there is something greater than what our eyes show us! Here, again, lies the Miracle of being mindful!

This connection (to the spirit) allows us to recognize with clarity some of the most basic things that happen around us every day. I spoke earlier about thinking with one of two thought-systems; those being one of **love** and **peace,** the other that of **fear and confusion**. We need to become aware of being <u>mindful</u>, so we can make the conscious choice to move with faith. Faith comes with a feeling of being connected that allows the "Holy Spirit" to work through us. Rather than us thinking that we are in control or know the answer. This is how miracles work. Miracles allow us to reawaken to the awareness of our spirits (not our body), and to receive the clarity of truth.

By this recognition, we will feel at peace in surrendering to our spirit. This will allow the miracle to adjust to our level of clarity and perception, so we may see it in proper alignment. This is what I believe all religions are designed to offer: the gift of love to our brothers and sisters of the world, because in spirit of God's vision, we are all one.

Being Mindful

What does it really mean to be mindful? Most people that I spoke with believe they are mindful. Some others thought that it meant being in the moment, as a good way of looking at how to be mindful. But how do we stay in such a "state of consciousness" all the time, in order for us to tell ourselves we are being mindful?

We must realize that the moment itself is fleeting (and can only be seen from the past in actuality). This means it needs further assessment for clarity to be understood. One of the most important things to look at when assessing <u>mindfulness</u> is where we are, and how we got there. However, most of us just follow the line (social conditioning or custom of our culture) and believe what we have been told about a particular thought-system. Most religions would have us follow a certain belief-system to give us a sense of right or wrong.

This is where we need to ask the question of ourselves, do our religions or our parents have the right answers for the things we do? The information passed on by our parents– was it the truth? Or did we just go along with it, and follow the patterns and conditioning of our parents? Do we really stop and look at what we say or do? I don't think so. We just find ourselves doing what we have always done, and that is to follow the patterns.

Mindfulness requires that we are <u>willing</u> to look at what we have become, and to the result of our choices. These choices have given us our direction and allows us to see where they have taken us. We must continuously assess the source of our direction and why we made those choices. This means that we need to surrender to our minds as the source and foundation of our choices. We must be willing to relinquish doing the same things over and over again (and calling it right, because it's a common pattern). Our willingness to examine our thoughts is where real change can be made, and clarity discovered. This is the source of mindfulness.

In our minds, we must recognize that we are the source, and that our behavior is only the result of our mind's direction. Our body is just there to carry out the wishes of our minds. Only the mind is capable of illumination, because only it has the capacities of continuous expansion. The body, on the other hand, is in a constant mode of decay and deterioration. It should be emphasized that the body does not learn any more than it creates. Remember, the body is just a medium or a learning device. It is our minds that allow us to share, and not our bodies. To recognize this is to have become mindful of our internal light, which can illuminate the body by allowing it to accept the mind as it creative source, and its internal light.

The Need For Assessment

Assessments is of great value in a mindful approach–in wanting to look at who we are. Without this mindful approach we will accept the illusions as real, and will endow them with our power, and give them value. This was the method we were taught and have believed to be valuable. We have let ourselves believe what we have been told and taught. But we were never told that our minds were the real source of our strength and our values are. We have always been led to believe that our bodies "ruled," and that it was the most important part of us. Yet, when we take a closer look at our body, we recognize that we can <u>not</u> make a directional change without our mind's input. This is another good reason to want to assess.

This should tell us that it is our minds which require our love and attention. When having a proper assessment, we come to realize that our body is but a learning device which helps us to communicate and learn. However, we also need to learn how to love, and how to become <u>one</u> in union. This is a process that happens through our thoughts (not our bodies). These thoughts drive our actions to crave and thrive on the need to associate with other like beings. They magnetically attract others like themselves, and with some intuitive understanding, they repel their enemies.

It is important for us when evaluating our <u>assessments</u>, to ask if we are just carrying out the family tradition, by doing what we were told. But these traditions and constant patterns have a tendency to groove our responses. These patterned responses have made us believe that we have chosen the right direction. And that this belief-system and patterns have now become an acceptable assessments.

These are the methods that science, religion, our parents and societies have used over long periods of time. They have encouraged us to believe what we were told, and not to question it. What this meant for us on a lot of levels was to give up our mindful understanding. But our mindful understanding was given to us–as a "natural gift of balance." Remember, there are only two major thought-systems that guide our thinking–one being that of <u>Peace</u> and <u>Love,</u> and the other is that of <u>Fear</u> and <u>Confusion.</u> This is imperative to look at these two systems with a mindful assessment.

Science is a process of curiosities and exploration; and it is important for us to understand its process. Science is about observation and evidence, and its acquisitions of data occurring in the past or as a projection into the future. By scientist compiling this data they are able to draw certain conclusions based on a given set of parameters (brought forth by their observation). This statistical data will give them a probable outcome in a given set of parameters, and then this becomes sound data. With the accuracy of these statistical observations, this material can become what we call truth and law. Thus losing sight of being mindful and becoming more likely to follow the line or pattern of our social conditioning.

Organized religion has approached this in a different way. It wants us to believe that our salvation is "out of our hands," and that we need the church to intervene on our behalf (if we are to be saved). This mind-set only creates more confusion, by us using a thought-system founded on fear—and not love. This will never bring us any level of clarity to the idea of love. We must realize that when our leaders are confused it would stand to reason that the followers would be equally confused.

If the "bibles" of the world have become our guides (our means and methods for understanding ourselves), we would think that the message would be clear and simple. However, that has not been the case for me. It has been anything but, and on many occasions quite confusing. There are many distortions about how to see the wholeness in ourselves by using a biblical approach. This method has kept us confused about what is really the Truth.

We must ask if it is wise to continue putting our faith in those that are knowingly confusing us about our union and our wholeness. In my thinking, the idea of the whole is quite simple. The whole represents oneness and union, and not separateness. When religion speaks of our brothers and sisters, it generally refers to them as members of its own congregation (and not to brothers and sisters of the world). This puts limits on the meaning of oneness and wholeness, doesn't it?

We have fought wars in the name of religion, yet religion speaks of peace. How could this reflect oneness or union? If we are allowing organized religion to tell us about God (our Creator), and the Godliness that is within us, this God, would have to be a part of all our brothers and sisters of the universe, right? God (our Creator) can only reflect the whole, and every one of us must reflect a part of that whole. Do you not agree?

Can God (our creator) only represent a small part of the whole?

God is love, and love is whole and never comes with contradictions. God can only reflect certainty, and never doubt. Doubt comes from misunderstanding or conflicts, which leads us to uncertainty and confusion. This will usually produce a split-mind, which creates more confusion about the direction we have chosen. With his dichotomy of thought, we cannot bring about a process of a mindful assessment.

Looking At Our Differences

If we cannot recognize the <u>spirit</u> of our brothers, then how can we see our own? It is my understanding that the essence of religion (as a spiritual process), is not to reflect on the differences we share, but to look at the union of our oneness.

Jill Bolte Taylor, Ph.D. and scientist tells us that as part of the human species we share all but 0.01 percent (1/100th of 1 percent) of identical genetic sequences. So, biologically, it tells us that as a species, we are virtually identical to one another at the level of our genes (99.99 percent). If we are ready to recognize this fact, we will then see the light that shines from within, and a natural connection to our brothers or sisters. Then we can recognize that we are all "Godly." This is God's gift. This gift of our union and oneness that we all share, and that gives us our <u>spiritual</u> <u>connection</u>. Isn't this the <u>love</u> that God would have us see?

The brothers and sisters we look upon will always be different in their physical appearance. Should that tiny part of u, stop us from loving one another? We find ourselves focusing on that small part of us that is different, rather than acknowledging how much we are alike. This is how we've become confused. By looking at such a small part, and making it enormous—thus distorting our reality. God (our Creator) does not see this difference.

Our Godly teacher teaches us to love thyself over all else, and to recognize and touch our own hearts. If we can recognize ourselves (and our own hearts), then, perhaps, we will want to touch our brothers and sisters as well. This indicates that we have made a spiritual connection. This connection creates our oneness and truth within us, and bring us peace. If we have found this connection it means that we can recognize our wholeness and our love of self.

Mindfulness is to assess, and this means that we are willing to examine and understand the event and what just happened. The understanding of that experience is complete and whole, and needs no input, only our evaluation.

Understanding Of Perception And Knowledge

Perception is the process of organization, identification and interpretation of sensory information. This allows us to fabricate a mental representation through the process of transduction. These are sensors in the body that transform signals from the environment into encoded neural signals. All perception involves signals in the nervous system. This, in turn, results from physical stimulation of the sense organs. This means that the body needs an object for comparison to have perception. For example, vision involves light striking the retinas of the eyes, producing an image. Our smell is mediated by odor molecules. Another example of this is when we walk into our mother's house and smell the aroma of our favorite food cooking, and we become hungry, even though we had just eaten. These are results of our odor molecules at work.

Perception is also based on our beliefs, and on what we have been told over the years. Every one of us has a belief-system, which is helping us interpret what it is we see, or understand what took place. However, when we do this, it is always <u>received</u> from a <u>perceived</u> notion, or from our past experiences. This information is never certain. To perceive is not to be certain. It only expresses and evaluates the objects or images that are in front of us. This is the process of perception. Perception also lends itself to the processing of time. And like time, our perceptions are always changing. This requires us to adapt to things that are changing all the time; and this is the process of perception.

To know (on the other hand), does speak to <u>certainty,</u> and can move without the confinement of any object or image. We have talked about the Truth before, in that the Truth—**just is**. As I've stated before, truth cannot be altered, and it remain the same Truth. Certainty is much the same way in that it is factual and comes with its own condition of peace——that makes it what it is! This is the basis for truth and love.

However, <u>misperception,</u> on the other hand, is riddled with fear, and fosters much confusion and uncertainty. It constantly wants us to reject the outcome, by having us misperceive what is right in front of us. This allows us to produce illusions and make them real. But when we look at certainty it requires nothing from us in order for it to be what it is. This leaves no room for misperception, because we are only assessing what is in front of us.

Knowledge is our creative thought-system, which gives us strength and clarity, and does <u>not</u> create actions of its own. It is also about certainty, and comes from the spirit of our being making us whole and complete.

Most perceptions are derived from our conditioning or patterns, which stem from the act of doing or being something. This gives our perceptions a physical realm to play in. And this usually makes our clarity and understanding clouded, and filled with judgment. Thus leaving us lacking in our understanding, and often fills us with fear and doubt.

Our perceptions are perceived at various levels. This makes most things look impossible, and our knowledge and understanding doubtful. Often this comes with the belief-system of judgment. Assessment comes with a continuous process of accepting and rejecting, or organizing and reorganizing what we see. The evaluation process is a critical part of our perception because it needs these reflective images for us to judge. This is what allows us to evaluate in the first place, telling us what it is we know.

My Mom told me a passage from the Bible, which states that "God created us in His image." And when I asked her what image is that, she spoke of Jesus Christ. I thought, yes, but was this the reflection of God's image. I also thought this could be a misinterpretation of God's message. Was this massage talking about our physical image or our spiritual one? Yet, many of us believe that God (our Creator) carries no physical image!

That being the case, who are we to say that God is not a German, English, Asian, Persian, African or Spanish? Wouldn't God be <u>all</u> of these cultures if God were to reflect our oneness? There can be only one (Creator) if we are all connected, regardless of what we choose to call our creator.

Love by its nature <u>can</u> only reflect itself. Like being tall or short, fat or thin, black or white, these are all part of the whole and can only reflect what it is. This is the gift of wisdom which is beyond our images of perceptions. To know is to be certain, and this is <u>beyond</u> perception.

How Do We Acquire Knowledge?

When we speak of knowing, we have to consider where "knowing" comes from. Is it something that we create, or is it something we merely observe? We must learn to accept or surrender to know or to be certain. This requires true perception–and nothing more is needed. Knowledge takes no real action of its own; it merely informs us of the thought-systems we are using at any given moment. This can be either the one of confusion and fear, or the one of clarity and understanding.

But knowledge itself performs no action of its own; it is like the Truth, (**it just is**). It is to be looked upon for sound direction, and to help us make our spiritual-connection.

The ironic part of this is that we believe that we create truth and knowledge. This makes knowledge something we believe we need to acquire----not realizing we already have it if we can surrender.

This is what God (our Creator) would have us see. When we speak of eternity, we must realize and accept swe are complete and whole, and eternity is always with us. By acknowledging our completeness, it help to get rid of the feeling of lack and the needy attitude. We will no longer fixate on our opposites or our differences. The importance of the color of skin, or the language spoken, will no longer have value. These thoughts all create internal conflict and not peace.

None of these thoughts are the will of God (our creator); because they are <u>not</u> about love or peace. They are but images of comparisons, and require our judgment. However, this is the process of our egos, which is under the domain of our physical bodies. It (our egos) requires us to use the thought-system that has us focus our attention on the differences, and not on "our spirit." But we must remember, we are more than just our bodies. We are <u>God's</u> <u>reflection,</u> and that is "our spirit," which is <u>beyond</u> the body and the physical realm as we understand it.

The Need To Surrender

To accept the idea of surrendering is for us to move beyond the process of being perceived as just the images of our bodies. This is where certainty is born, and where doubt no longer holds us captive. When we have accepted the idea of <u>surrendering</u>, we come to realize that there are no levels to process. Because to be certain (or to surrender) has only one direction, and it will always foster truth and love.

This process of having multiple choices quite often leads to doubt. And this method of thought usually fosters fear and confusion. Often this approach will have us see our brothers as our enemy, and tell us they cannot be trusted. So, if we cannot surrender or recognize this love and light in ourselves, how will we be able to see it others? To love is a natural process that we carry out every day.

To make the connection is to surrender to this love, and with this acceptance we can see that we are whole and complete. Our surrendering will not allow us to focus on the tiny part of us that make us notice our differences. Making the connection is about learning how to recognize and forgive our shortcomings. This will allows our spirits to tell us what our shortcomings are, rather than trusting what our eyes show us.

This does require some faith on our part, which also needs us to surrender to the experience. That experience cannot be seen with just our eyes—that is why it requires our faith. However, if we cannot surrender to our <u>faith,</u> it will then appear almost impossible to see true love. This lack of faith is nothing more than our denial of what is in front of us therefore keeping us focusing on what we want, rather than accepting what is there. Because, what is there, is all there is, anything else is but an illusion and cannot be real.

Faith

Faith is the process of internal peace, where all answers are waiting to be remembered and understood. For us to make our <u>spiritual connection,</u> it is imperative that we surrender to the idea that we are whole and complete. Our spiritual connection is about the oneness that exists all over the universe. With this connection we feel a bond, and a strength to our wholeness, which allows us to see the clarity and unity of our inner-light.

This light cannot be seen with our physical eyes, so we must be willing to surrender to a different vision— that of our spirit. The spirit is God's (our Creator) gift to all of us, so we may feel our connection.

We have seen and felt this connection many times before. When we look at a newborn child (even when we don't know him), we can still feel this connection. Or when we saw an animal get hit by a car, we felt it. When we meet a total stranger and feel that bond, this is about the connection. Faith is all about feeling our connection! Have you ever seen a TV program about helping children in other countries, and you felt compelled to help them? This is about our oneness that we are all share on some spiritual level.

Our spirituality can transcend time and space, and removes all obstacles from our path—if we can learn to surrender to our faith.

QUESTION: Why is it so difficult to see with our inner-vision?

Perhaps this comes from the idea that we believe we are just our bodies. We see this image in the mirror, and tell ourselves that is who we are. The other side of that coin is that we never had to process the idea of looking at ourselves with an inner-vision. This required for us to understand where we are and who we are. And quite often we do not even know the part we are supposed to be playing! This made it very difficult to have inner-vision without faith.

We find ourselves continuing this cycle for years. Then one day we wake up, to realize that we do not "call the shots." We are just here to learn how to be the best person we can be—and to love ourselves. If we look at ourselves with love, it becomes a difficult to look at others with any view other than the one of love. This view allows us to be in touch with our inner-vision.

When we are able to make this connection, we are honoring God (our Creator), because this is the source of our love. I spoke earlier about peace and love, and how they cannot be separated and that we cannot have one without the other. However, to believe that we <u>can</u> have this separation will produce nothing but chaos and confusion. It will keep us trapped in our old ways, imprisoning our own thoughts, and being terrified by what we have created.

Our acceptance is the key to the strength of our inner-self. That gives way to us becoming mindful, and this only requires for us to see what is in front of us. The process of having faith and surrendering—is all that's required in our willingness to not create illusions or false realities.

CHAPTER 7
Searching for Peace

I n searching for peace, I asked the questions: What does it really mean to search for peace? Are there special things needed? How do we actively look for something like peace? Or, can peace be an abstract thought that we just think about, but never really explored or understood. In talking with many people about the subject of peace, it seems to strike a chord as to what it means to have peace. Is the thought of peace but a figment of our imagination? Do I have to process something to find it? Could it be that it's already there just needing to be recognized to come alive for us?

Peace is like Truth–it only needs to be recognized for the glory of the moment to shine through. Part of the problem in trying to acquire anything is that we far too often start the journey with how difficult the task is going to be. This takes the joy out of the journey before it began. But the truth of the matter is that peace requires so little of us, it only needs to be recognized for it to be real. However, we often believe that we need to add something to the equation, so we may know it is of <u>our own</u> creation. This is where the confusion starts.

In searching for peace, we need only to recognize the Truth, and to accept that truth and love are one in the same. We must also recognize that truth is revealed, and <u>not created</u> by us or any other person. By choosing to acknowledge this as a conscious choice we have allowed ourselves to see what is in front of us. It is only in this acknowledgment that it makes the Truth what it is, and not what we wish it to be. Ask yourself this question, so you may examine it for yourself.

Ask if we can change the truth, then can it still remain the truth?

We can deny what is in front of us, but that does not change the facts of what <u>is</u> actually there. The denial is only our ego's way of telling us that we are the one who is right, which feeds the ego's need to be in control.

I have always thought of the Truth as, "*Just is,*–not mine, not yours, but "it just is." The proof of this process is that it is always right in front of us. However, can someone play a trick on us? Yes, they can, but this would be deception, and not the Truth at all. That would become just another illusion we have created. Illusions will always come from a place of confusion or our fantasies which ultimately lead to fear.

We have come to believe in our own arrogance that tells us we can establish our peace, and create truth– thus putting us in control. This is only our ego establishing its domain over our behavior of what it believes to be right and wrong. This establishes the ego's understanding of separate and different, where there actually are none. When we can accept our Godly understanding of ourselves as "spirits," we will recognize there is no difference or separation– only the reflections of our <u>union</u> and <u>oneness</u>. We will understand this is where peace resides, in our relationship with our brothers and sisters!

Recognizing Truth

Our understanding and recognition of Truth is critical in acquiring peace. This is a process of "getting out of our way," and allowing the Holy Instant to become what is Holy. This instant is not something we can create, it just happens when it is supposed to, (without the added arrogance to make it right). This instant is never seen in advance. It is only revealed after the fact, and that is what allows it to be holy. It is not from an external influence; it only comes from within (which is not to be seen, just experienced).

If we closely examine our actions we will see that we are often projecting into "tomorrow," and that is <u>not</u> what is in front of us. So, if we are living in our projections, that means we are not conscious of the experience or our next moment. Our projections are always made from an illusion which is "in our tomorrow," and not a part of the present. We have conditioned ourselves to believe that we can make the changes necessary to be at peace.

This allows us to confuse illusions with Truth, and have us accept that they are one in the same. By accepting this way of thinking we have come to believe that we can create our own truth. However, when we are willing to surrender to the Holy Instant, we will recognize that we did very little to bring about Truth. It was just given by the grace of our choice to listen to the inner-voice. We must realize that Truth doesn't come from us, but it is only revealed—through us. It is important for us to recognize how little our part was in what just happened, regardless of what it was. We project a lot in helping our ego to make us believe that we are in control, and that whatever we see is of our own doing. Thus, making us the architect of our truth—and our false peace and reality!

Here lies our confusion, and where fear is born. We must realize that we cannot hold a clear thought because time is continuous and fleeting. Yet, we want to believe that we can create the next thought with clarity. This is not true, because the next moment is always revealed (always fleeting), either through a thought, or through our actions. Is this not the truth? However, we never seem to get any lasting joy out of those moments, when we take charge or believe we are in control.

We began to have thoughts like: *it* could have been a little better; If it were only; but, if only; not quite yet; or maybe just a little more of this and little less of that. These are all thoughts of uncertainty and doubt about the right and wrong of our life, but none of these speak to Truth, certainty, or peace. Because the ego doesn't know of peace or truth, it can only tell us of the "idea" of peace or truth, which (again), is but a projection or illusion.

So, if we find ourselves in step nine or ten on our journey of life, perhaps we are just wishing or fantasizing, and not looking at what is front of us. God (our Creator) tells us that the Truth is *always, always, always* right in front us. It is never to be obscured by any images, and it is as clear as the light that brings dawn to our days. It is never to be hidden. Because, to hide it would be to confuse or deceive, and this is <u>not</u> God's way——or the way of universal Truth.

Realizing Freedom

Freedom is a process of letting go of our past, and to stop giving it our power and love. We must stop spending our time thinking about what happened yesterday, (or last month or last year), and all the possible consequences of what took place. This method of thinking will always keep us wondering what freedom is. The idea of freedom is born out of wanting to understand what really happened. The fact of the matter is that we only have a couple of options to choose from: it's either the truth, or it's not! It cannot be <u>both</u>, truth and false; it's either one or the other. Freedom comes from this understanding!

Truth has but one direction, and always travels with love as its companion. The ego (on the other hand) always walks with fear and confusion. Thus, the ego allows us to feel that sense of being complete or whole— and yet, there is something always missing! This creates a feeling of weakness and emptiness, and the feeling of being alone. When there is no understanding of what we are doing (and why we are doing it), we become confused by our own journey. Then, there will always be doubt about our decision and our direction. This approach never brings with it a feeling of resolve or peace—only more questions for which we have no answers.

We are all still searching for peace, and starting to realize that we are giving our power and our love away, when there is no return. Yet, in reality, that power and love would still exists within us. And, if that is the Truth, wouldn't this create a conflict inside of us? By knowing that if we have denied the given moment (over the direction we chose), then our reality could only be an illusion.

Clearer thinking is the path we want to take in becoming free. However, the process of clear thinking is always being bombarded with other thoughts— even those that do not appear to be in the right place. They just come up! And sometimes these same thoughts (in one form or another), leave us with the feeling of fear, hatred, pain, sadness and confused. By holding on to those thoughts of yesterday, we make them real to us "now." Because there is no answer for yesterday's questions, and yet we find ourselves, creating answers. These "created answers" could only be an illusion! Because we made them appear so real, we chose them over the Truth—— making them what we wanted them to be. Then, our actions create separation and aloneness.

Webster's dictionary tells us that to be free is to have a state of being free, or to be at liberty, rather than in confinement or under physical restraint. Looking at a deeper part of ourselves, can we realize that the same freedom is there, even if we were confined or physically restrained? And if we were able to really understand freedom, could we see ourselves also without limits? If we could see ourselves without limits, wouldn't that mean we are still free—— because our state of mind would still be free?

Webster's dictionary went on to include that freedom meant to be exempt from external control, interferences or regulation, etc. Could this mean that what is outside of us does not have a great deal of value, (and therefore) we should not be so attached to it?

We must realize that we are here to just observe the outcome. We can then acknowledge the event is over, and our focus is now on what we did see, rather than on what we wanted to see. By allowing input from the past to enter we have chosen to alter or interfere with the outcome. We are no longer just observing, but creating. We have learned to control by our own definitions. We have accepted that if we created the definition, we must believe in what we created. We then tell ourselves that this gives us the right to interfere with what we see–to make it our own. With this understanding, we give it (and us) limits. However, in reality, freedom is progressive and continuous, and is without limits–because we are free in "spirits."

Here, again, we must ask–can a definition define the spirit of freedom? We must come to recognize that freedom means to find our way through understanding and clarity. Freedom is not to be known as a word, or limited by a definition. It is only to be understood as a process of life itself!

A title, or definition of any kind draws us closer to the idea of what we have created. With our titles come definitions and limits. We continue to pull this all from our past. The past passes on great information to be processed. However, it is not to be held onto, and valued over our present. Yesterday will never be the same again. We do not need a definition if we are willing to process what is in front of us.

Freedom is derived from understanding, and not from feeling confused or fearful. How can we feel the presence of peace or freedom, without understanding? When we feel deprived of anything, we are feeling disconnected and alone. We are no longer aware of the wholeness, or that Holy Instant. Surrendering offers us clarity and understanding and we become sharper and more focused as we recognize our wholeness. By recognizing that we can not separate the whole, we realize that separation is but an internal conflict which is produced by our own fear and confusion.

It is important to recognize that freedom does not start from outside of us, and this brings us clarity, along with peace and understanding. This clarity is felt, rather than seen with our physical eyes. The physical world creates its own limits, and this world is governed by our ego. The ego can only interpret the external world and that which is outside of us.

The Ego Influence

The ego wants us to listen to its teaching, because then everything is presented as fragmented and separate. It does not allow us to recognize our own oneness, or to see our brothers or sisters as an extension of ourselves. This holds our brothers and sisters hostage (with our own self-centeredness), and never sees them or ourselves free. It is imperative that we be willing to forgive them, and ourselves——to be free!

Each lesson brings its own reward of being free. It allows us to see this freedom in our brothers' hearts, and to recognize it in our own heart, as well. The whole can never be destroyed—only denied. This denial will always produce major conflict in our minds. This conflict will not allow us to have peace with ourselves, or others. This denial will always keep us trapped, because we must be able to define what we created in order to make it real to us.

When we recognize this freedom in ourselves we can then accept that we do not create the next few seconds. With this insight, we are truly aware that we are <u>unaware</u> of what the next few moments are going to bring. Even though we had an input in making it what it is, that does not mean that we created it. However, our part did contribute to its wholeness. This is where being able to see what is in front of us is so important, by our willingness to recognize the Truth. This truth is always in front of us; not always seen–but always there! This is God's guarantee that Truth cannot be altered and still remain the Truth. Certainty cannot be uncertain–just like hatred cannot be seen as love. God wants us to know that if we start looking with the internal sight given to us, then we will recognize what is in front of us–and it will no longer be frightening.

We will feel the wholeness that we are–and feel the union of our oneness. There is no conflict in oneness, sameness or the whole. We must be willing to fight the urge to continue to do what we have always done. This willingness allows us to examine what is in front of us, without fear. This allows us to let go of our ego's influence and the confusion that comes with it.

Acceptance Brings A New Day

Acceptance needs us to allow ourselves to receive the moment, that Holy Instant where we can experience the certainty and connection to our spiritual self. In this instant, we recognize truth and peace and know that we have already received them. By recognizing this Holy Instance in ourselves we also start to see it in others. We all carry innocence, this feeling of being without guilt. However, we find it hard to accept that we can be guiltless. We have accepted the definitions that we have been told for so long, as to who we are, and this story has always come with guilt.

With our acceptance of love of our self, we come to understand that we are never alone; and with this clarity, life starts to enhance its blessing. With these graces, we want to forgive and reconnect willingly with our spiritual self. To focus on this love is what we will choose to share: this will be the reflection of God's love. The willingness to share this love, at any moment in time, with anybody, is the reflection of God's blessings.

When we start to feel that oneness within us (and that feeling of wholeness), a change takes place. This is like a connection to <u>faith;</u> an awareness we have never experienced before, a feeling so special we are not even aware of how we got there. Wherever that may be! The where is not important, because this is the gift of acceptance, which allows us all to come together to "realize our oneness." The thought of this can become difficult only when we deem it so, by the denial of our union, which is in front of us.

This action is always preceded by fear, guilt and confusion. This denial produces uncertainty and doubt, and the poor decisions that follow. These decisions never lead to peace, just more fear and confusion. This leaves no room in our hearts for love or forgiveness. We will no longer be able to see what is in front of us. Our fear would become so intense that we are only capable of seeing what we want—— not what is there. This is nothing but our projections or desires of a particular outcome that we want to see. This is not acceptance, but denial, and only confused conflictions can come of this.

Acceptance is about allowing ourselves to remember that we have a spiritual connection, and with the desire of its presence, we have God's presence in our lives. This connection is about understanding the concept of eternal and forever—— this lasting light that shines within us all. The understanding of Truth is that this eternal light was given to all of us, as a part of our <u>birthright</u>. This is what is meant by the terminology " the light of eternalness and forever lasting light." God (our Creator) glows within us all. Thus truth can <u>not</u> be changed or altered, nor can this <u>eternal light</u> ever go out!

Acceptance naturally flows to the direction of patience, which is also an important part of seeking peace. Patience requires that we examine what is in front of us. Patience brings with it the clarity to recognize that the ego is but an illusion in our minds, and this will confuse us as to our true identity. When we look upon our brothers of the world we will notice that we all look different. However, at our spiritual level—— we are all the same!

The ego doesn't have an answer for this for us. Yet, the Truth is always right there in front of us. However, if we are looking for the Truth in any other place, it would only bring about a perpetual illusion, making it what we want it to be rather than accepting what it is.

Faith

If we accept the idea that there can be <u>multiple</u> truths we will also believe we can alter the truth and it still remains truthful. What was right in front of us has now been changed. We made it different for our own benefit! Here, again, we have created separation, not union. The ego likes to play tricks like this with our minds because it has the understanding that if it lets us realize who we <u>really</u> are, it would be to its own detriment.

The ego plays off the errors of our brothers and sisters and would have us attack them over the mistakes they have made. This makes us believe that the errors are of great value. The ego wants us to pass on judgment and punishment as the price we must pay for our mistakes. With this conflict inside of us, how would we ever see our brothers as an extension of ourselves? This approach will never allow us to recognize the peace within them.

Faith (like peace) can only come from one source. The understanding of the source comes through our clarity and understanding of nature, and this can only happen by our invitation to have peace as our source. The idea of coercion does not apply here. We must develop faith as a guide to our decisions, rather than being co-erced by outside sources. For us to truly accept, we must have Faith, because the way we have learned to receive is all so different. We need faith to process it for us. Faith produces healing, and healing is a way to release the dangers and fears that our ego brings to our door every day. By recognizing this Truth in us we allow ourselves to recognize it in our brothers–as we give this healing, so are we healed! These are God's (our Creator) Natural Laws! However, we need Faith to accept these Natural Laws.

Why Do We Choose Illusion Over Truth When The Truth Has Already Been Revealed?

In speaking about truth in a spiritual philosophy kind of way, we have to look at the separation we made between truth and illusions. These terms may be real or unreal for you. While these terms are both valid distinctions in themselves, they cannot be applied to describe the manifestation of our world. They can only validate a description of our perceptions. The term illusion is a good example of our poor perception, and can only reflect a poor understanding. This implies the depth of our confusion and our fears, and with this reflection comes a true lack of understanding of who we are.

Truth is also a perception, but one of depth, which allows us to perceive <u>more</u> of what is there. This allows a connection to be made and it brings clarity to what we see. This is not something that we can call upon (to make it what we want), and yet, our participation is critical for truth to be revealed.

On the other hand, illusions are but a tiny glimpse (or a small fragment) of truth, producing poor perception of what it is we believe we see. This is normally driven by our desires for something, and is most often different from what we see in front of us–thus making it a fantasy, and not real at all. From this superficial level of perception we will often experience separation, anxiety, and disconnection–creating a feeling of aloneness and fear. This produces the need for the terms: "I," "Me," "Mine." This creates the need for multiplicity (the need to have many things), and the need to alter the truth. Freud called this our alter "Ego."

At our deeper levels of awareness we experience union and oneness. It is through our spiritual connection that our perception changes and we start to experience a deeper level of understanding. We start to understand who we are and what the things around us really mean, and in that instant we find our connection–and Truth is revealed. This goes beyond the form of our appearances, and beyond any level of things or objects that are before us. This is why in many philosophies, the world "of form" is often called the "world of illusions."

The source or existence of anything or anyone is but a unique reflection of that source, or essence. Each contains both universal dimension and the individual dimension. It is the universal dimension that all life and all beings are linked together. So, therefore, if this statement were true (which I believe it is), then, truth is always unifying in its effects.

Illusions, on the other hand, are driven by fantasy, making that which is real fit the dream of what we wanted it to be. The Ego is the master of illusions, and we help to maintain its power. For this reason, it will always demand our allegiance. When we look at illusion closely we will find that it is always driven by thoughts of the past, or a projection of our future. Neither of these is real, and yet we make this choice. Peace can never be found in the confused actions we take; these actions can only produce further confusion. The past is gone (and cannot be changed) and the future has not yet arrived. And yet, we find ourselves struggling to find peace and love in a place–where it cannot be found.

Discovering The Influence Of Our Egos

To find love or peace, we must start first by recognizing the love from within ourselves–here is where true love resides. When we follow the teaching of our ego (or just trust in illusions), we will not have a clear answer to any question that we asked. It is important that we remember the ego cannot produce any clear answers. It can only alter our perception and have us believe in a false truth. However, to alter perception does not produce truth. But, if we have bought the idea that multiple truths are possible, then (in our minds), we can make it fit–thus making it acceptable.

With this understanding, we believe we can change the past, and by so doing, this is where we will live our lives–in the past. If we are living in the past, this will not allow us to recognize the present or Truth. The Truth always reflects the **present** or **now,** and will not be concerned with yesterday, or the projection of tomorrow. Yet, this is where the ego wants us to reside. This approach will keep us confused and without love or peace in our lives. How is it that the ego can memorialize us, and keep us trapped in the past? The ego continuously tells us that this is where our power lies, and where we are in control. But if we notice the outcome of our actions, no real change ever takes place.

If we let our minds reflect back, we will see how much of our time is spent in the past. The past is gone never to return again. However, for some of us, this is where we feel we have the greatest amount of control over our lives. This could be just our fantasy, or our illusions. Our deeper understanding tells us the truth. This is with great disapproval from our ego, because the ego demands <u>obedience</u> to its direction. This is our conditioning from our childhood programming. It wants us to believe that yesterday is valuable and we should hold on to it. This is a very different direction from the one passed on by our spiritual self. It moves in the totally opposite direction than that of our ego. We must come to understand that even though we have both directions at our finger tips, we are still choosing one over the other— making a choice between Truth and illusions. It is very important that we are conscious of this distinction and the choice we make between the two.

This brings us to a place where we recognize if we are choosing truth over illusions, or the other way around. This place that we recognize can only be the present, here and now; any other place would be made from an illusion–and could <u>not</u> be real. Think about that for a second, and you will realize it could be no other way.

Yes, we are being asked to let go of our past. However, we still have to process those emotions, before we can let them go. Our old programming and social influences wants us to hold on to those old principles of judgment and separation. With this approach, we are not reminded of those thoughts of forgiveness and love. We are all trying to understand our brothers, but maybe we are going about it from the wrong direction. We can only see the difference, and not our sameness as an appropriate directional choice.

Remember, our individual dimension looks at us from a superficially small and even fragmented point of view. If we can not get beyond this mode of thinking, how can we see the blessing that we receive every day? Every person we meet is there to help us recognize our authentic-self. This allows us to realize who we are; and not who we want to be.

Do We Understand Our Decision?
Question: When we make our decisions, do we understand <u>why</u> we made that decision?

I ask this question because I think most decisions are <u>not</u> made with love or understanding. They are made out of fear and confusion, and never with unity. Think about all those friends we know that have stayed in a bad relationship, which they knew was not healthy or good for them. Yet, when we ask, "Why are you staying?" they respond that they don't know, or give an answer that is crazy or unclear. Is this not confusion? Or, when friends tell us that they have a great investment with a particular company, and they often fail to tell us of the bad things they have heard about that company. Wouldn't that be a devious and deceitful act in any business dealing?

These same people go forward with that company and they take a great loss. Did they see or sense the warning sign given to them by their spiritual self? No, they generally deny what they felt. They move forward, which allows them to respond with more confusion.

When we are with a group of friends and they are attempting to do something that is harmful and disgraceful to another human we might even allow ourselves to go along with it, out of some misplaced fear. Later, we tell others what a bad thing they have done. Even though we did nothing personally, we stood by and did nothing to stop it. Isn't this an action of fear? So, how can we tell ourselves that we are conscious of our decision?

Let's say we have a partner, mate, or a significant-other that we are afraid to talk to. They always need to be right. They often attack us verbally or physically if we disagree with them. This can produce some issues of poor self-esteem or even major fear. So, if we don't understand our decisions, then, how can we be at peace with them, or ourselves?

Taking A Stand

It is often easier for us to just go along, rather than make waves by stepping out of line. Yes, we can take this approach, but does this make it any less confusing or less fearful for us? This conflicted question has always kept us confused and tends to make us recognize the illusions as real. Illusions are never about real or clarity, but they are always about fear and confusion.

To take a stand has its own level of discomfort, for sure. However, we must look at pain and ask if the pain or discomfort has a greater value than the outcome that it reveals. The pain of a particular affliction can be worth the experience of the pain. Take, for example, a young women or wife that chose to have a child. She accepted that pain and discomfort would be a part of her journey. It is possible that the joy or blessing of having a child far outweighs the pain.

We must ask ourselves if we understand our own motives to our responses, or to our thoughts. Usually, the answer is no. If this is our answer, how can we be at peace or have the willingness to share love? If the principle for making our decision (or directing our motive) is <u>not</u> made out of love, then, how will we ever feel connected? No decision made out of love can be conflicted! We must remember that our acceptance is only there to be observed– not created. Our decision to love helps us feel at peace and to be without conflict with our brothers.

How will we ever understand the principle of our oneness or sameness when all that we see is difference and separation? Wouldn't this mean there must be a polarity in our thoughts, and thus, a winner and a loser? How would this bring us peace in taking this stand or position?

Values, How Do We Acquire Them?

Values can be defined as broad preferences concerning appropriate courses of action, and yielding to a particular outcome. As such, values reflect a person's sense of right and wrong and what "ought" to be. This is but a projection, and has no level of certainty or rightness about it. This also implies (or would have us believe) that <u>rightness,</u> should have a particular outcome. This puts us on a roller-coaster of uncertainty about most of our decisions, and this will not allow our own values to bring us any level of peace.

This is because we believe that our value-system should have a predictable outcome. However, a predictable outcome requires a projection into the future, and since the future is really unknown, a predictable outcome is usually unknown and, in actuality, it is just an illusion.

At our spiritual level love has just <u>one</u> direction. It shares this connection with everyone and everything, carrying with it peace and truth, and it cannot be altered, changed, or separated. The whole is complete, just like us. The real value is to recognize this as Truth.

According to Morris Massey, values are generally formed during three significant periods: (1) Imprint period from birth to 7 years, (2) Modeling period from 8-13 years, (3) Socialization period from 13-21 years.

Personal values provide an internal reference for what is good, beneficial, important, useful, beautiful, desirable, constructive, etc. According to Morris Massey values generate our behavior and help solve common problems for survival, by comparative ranking of the values. The result of this provides answers to questions of why people do what they do, and in what order they choose to do them. Over time, these personal values become public values. This transition formed the foundation of laws, customs and traditions.

Personal values (in a collective sense), become cultural values, either in agreement with or divergent from prevailing norms. A culture is a social system that shares a set of common values, in which such values permit social expectations, and collective understanding of the good, beautiful, constructive, etc. Here again are illusions looking right at us, and, yet, we choose not to see them. Because, if we are projecting, we are not willing to receive, and, if we look at our track record on getting what we asked for, our percentage would be a very low number. How often have we really obtained just what we ask for? We, indeed, always receive an outcome, but, often it is quite different from what we had planned.

This is about receiving, not projecting. If the value system that we received is not based on love, how could we ever see the same in that which is different? Every brother and sister of the planet will always appear as different. Even when they are identical twins, they will still appear with differences. So, how do we see the same in that which appears to be different? We must see the love that they carry, as a part of their birthright (given by God, our Creator). If we can see this love in ourselves, it becomes quite easy to recognize it in others. In this approach there is never a loser, because in the oneness or same, there is no conflict.

However, to understand this approach, we must be willing to receive the experience. We must understand what we are being told, rather than just projecting a particular outcome. The projection always has us scrambling, confused, and uncertain about our next step. How could we find peace in a constant state of confusion? Is this even possible, some have asked? We have to look at what our parents and the social influence of our society have passed on, and ask if these are the values that we want to hold onto. We must recognize these "established values" have many serious flaws, and often do not pertain to changing conditions. We must take a stand by becoming mindful of our decisions and our values.

Restoring Faith

Most of us like to think that we can function very well from both sides of the fence. Yet, we find ourselves wondering, why we can not find any level of happiness or peace from our choices. Remember, we spoke earlier about how God said that the Truth is always, always, always, right in front of us! We need only our willingness to accept this Truth: what is in front of us is our reality, and our truth. It is just that simple. Truth is always simple, and maybe this is because simple is always clear, concise and without confusion.

However, the key to restoring our faith is in our willingness to accept the idea of one direction (which is that of love), without any alteration or substitutions. This one direction is that of love. But our ego usually will not allow our acceptance of the thought-system without a challenge, because our happiness and joy is not of any major concern to our ego. We must also understand that the ego is quite clever, and will disguise its motives to gain our trust and make us believe it is our ally. With this internal betrayal of our self, to ourselves, this leaves us filled with anxiety and confusion about the next step in restoring our faith.

The Holy Instant is God's gift of restoring faith, by allowing us to receive that moment, without judgment. This moment (by its very nature) is the Truth, and reflects reality as it is. This instant lets us see our brother or sister for who they are, and also as our teachers, and "our guiding light." We need to learn that we are the perfect students if we can function without judgment or conflict. With this understanding of our oneness, we can then acknowledge our experiences, which lets us feel our Godliness. However, this does require our Faith!

Faith cannot be seen. It can only be <u>felt,</u> and needs our invitation to that moment to be experienced! The more we allow the experience of faith to take place, the more blessings we will receive. They will become our God-like reflections, or miracles. These reflections (sometimes called miracles) are just our awareness of being mindful of the moment. To surrender to this kind of internal faith allows us to look at what is in front of us, and to recognize its clarity, without fear or judgment.

The book, A Course in Miracle, states that way, a miracle is only the Truth made clear, and that to be mindful is merely to understand the direction we have chosen. This makes our choices clear, and our goals understandable, so they may be accomplished. Faith does require us to have such a focus and concentration on the task at hand. This will ensure that we do not allow other things to interfere with the accomplishment of our goals.

In talking with some friends on the subject of faith, I asked them what they thought faith was, and you can image some of the answers: Here are a few:

- From a friend that has a scientific background, he thought faith exists in opposition to our rationalistic thought-system.
- To others, it was to have confidence in a person or thing (e.g. I have faith that my brother will keep his promise)
- Many believed in a proposition or a belief system without proof (e.g. " I have faith in God ")

We must be willing to take small steps when it comes to restoring faith, until we understand what faith is to us. Faith can <u>not</u> be seen, and no one can really tell us what it is about. Because no one can give us a clear definition of faith——it must be felt!

Like the Holy Instant, we don't know when it is coming——it just shows up! But, it is our recognition of this Truth that allows us to have faith—— and learn to walk with peace. Those things we understand, we do not fear. With this acknowledgment we can have peace and clarity—— and with this, a restored faith.

Making Our Connection

Our spirit always experiences the situation as a whole—— because the whole is all there is. This implies that truth and clarity are always there, and with them, peace, to make it complete and whole. There is nothing else needed. However, our spirit needs our faith to accomplish this process. If it is that our goal is to see the whole and the truth, then we will move beyond the deceptions of any kind (fantasy or illusion) that stand before us.

When a situation is experienced, and is <u>not</u> whole, we often recognize it as a fragment, which always appears as a separate entity. This, then creates an illusion for us. With this approach, we can never experience the whole truth. Truth calls forth faith, and faith encumbers truth. This requires any goal of truth to be one with faith, and the whole.

Any relationship that is shared with the Holy Spirit is one of wholeness, and will no longer allow us to feel loneliness, even when we are alone. This means that we have made our spiritual connection with ourselves, and with our brothers. We have moved beyond the idea of I or Me, and have now changed our focus to register the We. Then, we can allow ourselves to share the love we have found inside of ourselves. This is our love connection, which moves in only one direction. When we recognize that this love is to be shared by all of us, we then acknowledge that love and whole are one.

Question: Why are we so challenged to accept any man or woman as our brother or sister?

Maybe it's because in a physiological way, they look different. Maybe it's because they were born from different parents. We have been told that they could not be our brother or sister for a number of reasons. Perhaps, it's because they speak a different language, or come from another country. Could it be that our skins are of a different color, and we have made this a sound criterion for us to not accept them as our brothers?

These are all possibilities, right? But we need to ask ourselves if any of those responses reflect a God-like connection! The last I heard was that we are all children of the world, and, we are God's children! God's children reflect no color; they come from no particular mother or father; nor do they speak any particular language. Our spiritual connection is beyond the physical body as we know it.

We must be willing to experience the spirit of us, and learn to see with a different vision. Here again, we need to ask if we are willing to let go, and walk with faith! If so, we may experience that holy instant as it unfolds in front of us.

There is nothing hard about having faith. The problem is in what we have been told about faith. We have been told we are in control, and the thought of letting go of that control brings on fear and anxiety. We have not been able to recognize that this is only our ego standing in our way. It tells us what it has always told us, that this connection cannot be made, and faith is not real. Yes, the ego wants our attention, just like our spirit does. The difference is that the ego demands sacrifice in every step we take. Our spirit merely asks that we invite it in, so it may connect us with what is already there. There are no sacrifices needed, and no demands made.

What happens when we recognize that sacrifices no longer have value, and we choose to remove them from our way of thinking? To make a sacrifice of anything is to give up something. That means that someone would be weakened by giving, and there is a possibility that someone else is gaining from the exchange. It is also my understanding that in sacrifice (as we know it), there is also a bit of suffering that takes place. This could also bring on an element of guilt as a part of the sacrifice. All these approaches reflect the methods of the ego. They keep us confused about the process of finding our connection, and about our love for one another.

Compassion-How Do We Recognize It?

It's hard to have true compassion in our hearts when we are carrying sacrifices and guilt around with us. This could only lead to internal confusion. How could this be a good place to be? Where is the love in this approach? There is no love there. And there will never be love because this is the approach of our ego. The ego wants us to believe that sacrifice and suffering are needed to love. This is but an illusion, if there ever was one. When we connect with our spirits, there is no weakening of our system. There is no sacrifice made because our oneness cannot be different. What I want for myself, I also want for you, as well. Here, there is no sacrifice, and no suffering is needed.

The meaning of all things will be reflected in its wholeness, and in the universe. Without the universe joining us we could not be complete and whole. This connection and unity of our brothers-----is but a gift of love. It is an acknowledgment of our compassion that we all make up the whole. However, if we have acquired the belief of sacrifice, then someone has to lose, and someone also has to pay.

With this thought process, we must limit ourselves to the physical body as a means of joining. When we can make our spiritual connection, we will be able to touch our Godliness, and then we are given a new way of seeing our bodies. We will look at a situation with clarity and peace, and without limits or sacrifice. We will find that we are connected to the Holy Instant, which brings forth unity and compassion. The Holy Instant transcends the meaning of sacrifice (or the need for guilt), because it allows us o see the gift of love. At this instant, a reflection of the universe is being shared, and that reflection is our reality.

Question: Does the situation provide our outcome, or does the truth reveal the outcome?

First, let us look at how we go about assessing a particular situation or outcome, and then, what is our method for deciding which direction we choose to take. There are several reasons to assess the situation before embarking on a road untraveled, when looking for unknown results. Most situations are represented in many different ways, but will only give us two options to choose from: one being that of <u>Love</u>, and the other that of <u>Fear</u>. We make most of our decisions based on these two choices. Love, reflecting truth and clarity, gives us our one direction approach to what we have chosen. The other is Fear, which produces confusion and chaos, and never reveals a clear answer to the choice we made. This approach will never allow us to have peace or happiness because this is not a part of fear's make-up. One of the first things we need to understand is to know to what degree we are confused:

- The first thing needed is to identify the magnitude of our confusion to the problem we are facing.
- We must also look at any situation as a means of understanding, and recognize that any situation is there for our growth.
- We also recognize that only the minds can join, and not the bodies.
- Our connection is imperative for sound communication to take place.

When we are identifying our confusion, it is important that we look at what is in front of us, because nothing else is real–at that moment. Having said that, most of us do <u>not</u> want to look at what is there, because we are fearful. Our willingness to accept what we have been told has created many problems for us, by just accepting what is not there. Usually, this leads to poor understanding of what is there, thus creating a poor assessment of the direction we choose.

Compassion As A Joining Of Minds

We also need to recognize that things just don't happen and there is meaning behind our actions (even when we are not aware of them). In our assessing the situation, we will discover that understanding can only lead to our growth. This can only happen if we allow our compassion to shine, and this only happens by our invitation. This means there can be no conflict. Where clarity is revealed, understanding becomes quite simple. We must realize the body cannot assess, it can only follow orders—and our minds give those orders.

It becomes imperative for us to allow ourselves to recognize our <u>minds</u> as the director of peace and faith. Sound communication and joy come by the joining of the minds. This allows our ideas to be exchanged, and helps to release us from our fear of feeling trapped. When we can see only part of a situation or circumstance it is hard to have any level of clarity. This fragmented thought will always lead to fear, doubt and confusion. This is what happens when we merely accept our conditioning (and the misdirection of our egos), rather than forming a sound plan of action.

Many people have told me that they create their own outcome. They believe they create their own realities and thus are able to determine their own faith. How does any person in any situation determine their outcome? If we try to make an informed decision with only part of the information, how much clarity will there be in our decisions? We have been told for years to move with only a small part of the equation, and, yet, we often make critical decisions about our directions with only a fraction of information.

We must be willing to surrender to something greater than ourselves. Here again lies the greatest confusion of all——to believe only what we have been told. We must be willing to surrender (and trust that inner-voice inside us), when things are not quite what they appear to be.

What Does It Mean To Surrender To Our Greater Power?

We must allow ourselves to experience what just happened, rather than telling ourselves what we wanted to happen. We must ask ourselves if we alter the truth does it still remain truthful? Many people think it does. But this leads me to wonder what truth would look like under such circumstances. If the truth is to reflect what is in front of us, how could we alter it and have it remain the same? Here is where the bewilderment takes place: we want peace, but only on our own terms. This assumes we created peace or truth in the first place!

It is my understanding that peace and truth come to us by the grace of God. We only need to welcome them (peace and truth) into our hearts. This is the process of acceptance, we need to recognize that faith, peace and love require nothing more than a welcoming invitation. And if there is more than that required, we are adding our own "two cents," and that is often too much.

Love and truth need only our intent of heart to be extended, to be pure and without conflict. Our intent will tell us the direction we have chosen for ourselves and our brothers. When we look at our intent with authentic assessment we receive a reflection of ourselves. With our proper intent of heart, there is always a "win, win" attitude for all concerned. There can be no conflict in the same or a one direction approach.

What Does It Feel Like To Be Connected?

We have all experienced this connection before with God, our Creator. I have been told that God speaks to all of us, all the time. We just fail to hear our inner-voice and choose our own desires, rather than using the guidance that is being given to us. Our universal connection is a natural part of us. If we continue to deny its presence our joining will <u>not</u> be recognized, and we will lose sight of our Godliness.

Yes, this could bring on a strange and new sensation, because we have become afraid of letting ourselves "feel." The fear of not being able to look at some part of ourselves creates barriers in our minds and a fear of what we might find. However, until we can open this door to our fears that part of ourselves will not have any level of sustained peace.

Remember, love always starts from within, at the source. This connecting source is our Holy Spirit, which we all possess. It gives us that feeling of not being afraid, and recognizes that we are never alone or separate. It give us a feeling of moving <u>beyond</u> our bodies. It is like creating a piece of music, and not remembering how you created it, and yet it turned out to be beautiful. That is the feeling of being connected!

It is difficult for us to acknowledge that we don't understand what happened, when we were there every step of the journey. This identifies that our physical sight has become lacking. We are starting to recognize that we are seeing with a different level of clarity and with a new internal vision. We begin to have answers to some of life's most difficult questions, and yet we are not aware of how we received these answers. We never really have an understanding of how we know or what we know. This is what it would feel like to be connected.

This is all about surrendering to our Godliness that connects us all. This connection is rooted in love, and is always <u>without</u> conflict or confusion. Love can only reflect the whole, or the union that we all share. The whole can only be one. Only when we alter the whole can we derive many.

Surrendering, What Does It mean?

When we surrender to a new thought-system, it will require some faith. This new thought system will go against everything our eyes have told us was real, and that can be frightening. But don't fret. When we surrender, we will start to trust ourselves, and there will be a shift in our confidence and clarity. Things will appear to us in perfect order, and with sound understanding. There will be a peace given to us which will feel strange and beautiful all at the same time.

We all have had glimpses of this energy; we just don't know what to make of it, and how to apply it in our life. We have called these experiences "miracles," because we cannot explain them. I truly agree with that assessment. The key question is, how can we stay in this place where these miracles are happening? This can only happen through the process of surrendering.

We must become mindful of who we are and where we are. Then, we will start to be mindful of our brothers and sisters of the world. Why do I keep bringing up the connection? It's because only in <u>spirits</u> can we have this connection, and it is important for us to remember that bodies cannot join, or become our union. Our bodies cannot have a reflection of oneness. So we must get beyond the body of our brothers, to touch his or her spirit. This can only happen through the joining of our spirits, or making that connection. This is more than just a word or a phrase. This is about our willingness to surrender to the Holy Instant, which reveals all Truths, and always travels with the companion of love.

The brothers and sisters of the world are our teachers, and we are the students. But we must learn to listen with our <u>hearts</u> (not our ears), to hear their pure intent of heart. When we become mindful, we will start to understand what we are being asked by our brothers. We will no longer be afraid of these questions because we have come to recognize that he is only asking for love.

When we answer any question with love, we will always be responding with understanding, not confusion. Remember, we are always responding with one of two choices: that of <u>love</u> or that of <u>fear</u>. These are the only two choices we ever make; they just appear differently. A choice made from fear might result in anxiety, depression, chaos or many other things that we thought were valuable and real.

Let us look at fear for a second and see how fragmented it really is. Its appearance will change many times to keep us confused about what it is we see. This will continue to have us project this fear that we feel within ourselves on others. This holds us in a past experience and keeps us fearful. Often these results made from fear might come disguised as anxiety, depression, anger or many other forms of emotions that we have made valuable.

Love, on the other hand, brings forth clarity and truth. With love our choice of direction and goals will be accomplished, because our focus is clear, and our minds are without conflict.

This is the nature of Love. Love cannot be defined with words, or put in a box to be what we want it to be. Love is like us: dynamic and forever changing, like reality itself.

As my dear friend Nettie would say, "Love just is"

CHAPTER 8
Recognizing our Oneness

Awareness

In wanting to recognize anything, we first must be aware of its presence. We must allow ourselves to experience what is there. Awareness is to be conscious of the moment, regardless of what has taken place. Sometimes, I have asked myself, what is it that I am truly aware of, and I then realize that it isn't very much. Often, we try to make things fit the outcome so we can have our needs met for the moment. We go on to tell ourselves that it is ok, because it is what we created. When in reality, it was just an outcome that fit our needs for that particular circumstance. On many other occasions, the outcome brought on anxiety and stress that fueled our confusion, anger or depression.

This keeps us with internal conflict, and a lack of awareness of what we choose <u>not</u> to see. This confusion keeps us wondering if we can continue to make the substitutions necessary to make things appear as we would like them to be (never really under-standing why). Substitutions, by their nature, require that we make a change to what is there. We do this all the time, consciously or unconsciously. When we are conscious of our actions, it becomes an act of awareness and a mindful understanding of the experience or events. On the other hand, when we act with un-consciousness, it means we can make substitutions, and then tell ourselves that it fits, to make it feel okay. It could also mean that we deny that this event ever happened and this would make it our truth or our reality.

I wonder if this could ever be awareness, for us to deny the truth that is right in front of us. How could we ever feel the oneness of our awareness in such an approach? To be aware is quite simple, really, it only requires that we take in the event. This only appears hard or difficult when we believe we are in control, or crave the need to be in control. Often this approach leads us to denial or substitutions, which cannot lead to awareness or oneness ——only more confusion.

Clarity Of Thought

Clarity of thought will always come about when we recognize what has just taken place. So, by not allowing ourselves to make the judgments about the right or wrong of an event we merely look at what actually happened. By doing this, we give ourselves time to hear our inner-voice for the clarity it brings. Clarity, by its nature, always comes without distortions or conflict. These concepts could not be a part of clarity. They must be a part of confusion, which always travels with distortion and fear as its companion.

Remembering ourselves without the limits of fear and confusion is very difficult for many of us. We have been conditioned to accept these limits, as to who we are. These are the limits that we have chosen to accept, and this has created a great deal of fear and confusion about who we are. This has created a foundation for our separation from one another by not allowing us to recognize our spirits— and our oneness.

By accepting and remembering our spiritual connection we can start to live without some of those limits that are brought on by our fears and judgments. These thoughts of fear and judgment go on all the time and we cannot stop this process. However, we can remember to surrender to the process, thus creating a smoother passage to the same direction. Where there is no internal conflict, the path is always smoother. Then our balance will be naturally restored, with little or no effort required on our part. Nature will always adjust its course to balance the use of our universal laws. We only need to learn how to release the images of being in control. We will then allow ourselves to love— and to surrender to being loved! This is what clarity is all about, <u>acceptance</u> without the need for control.

This will, then, become our path to compassion and to peace. When we are willing to surrender to this approach we have also removed some of our limitations. This allows us to remove some of our fears. Fear paralyzes us in that it keeps us wondering about tomorrow, rather than experiencing the now-moment. It paralyzes us to an outcome that is not visible, regardless of how well we plan the event. Our fears continue to mount and create chaos around us, which does not allow us to have peace.

Discovering our clarity is a critical part of finding our compassion and love for oneself. When we can give up the judgments of ourselves it becomes easier for us to not judge others. This is the process of recognizing our oneness and our clarity.

Acceptance

When you think about the process of acceptance, what comes to mind for you? Many, of us experience acceptance as a difficult task. This could be because we believe that something is required from us in order to have this acceptance. This make us believe we need to add something to the experience. Acceptance requires so little from us that it makes some of us nervous. It confuses us, because we believe that something more is needed to make it complete.

Yet, the only thing that is required from us is an <u>authentic</u> <u>assessment</u> of what just took place (nothing more or nothing less).

Life is a process of transition, and this never stops. To process this idea without a continuous level of internal conflict we must learn how to accept. It is a natural act for us to accept. However, we have been taught not to accept, but to be alert or in control, or to believe we can be in control. But, the fact of the matter is that we can <u>not</u> control nor predict the next few seconds with any level of certainty.

Then, the key to <u>acceptance</u> is to allow ourselves to surrender and to not be put off by what might happen next. Remember there are no coincidences, which means there is something to be learned and gained by what just happened.

Surrendering is only difficult when we want to be in control of the outcome. When we allow our projections to take over, we then want what we want and when we want it— and this is control! There will never be peace that comes with this type of projection. It only creates more conflict and confusion. Any approach that is founded on fear and projections will always have an uncertain and chaotic outcome.

Surrendering does require a bit-of-faith. It allows us to drop some of the limits and restrictions of our growth. By being able to drop some of these limits we let go of some of the constraints that restrict our being. This allows us to recognize our spiritual connection and the balance that comes with this re-connection. This balance provides us with a new foundation of peace within ourselves, and with others. However, this connection requires that we accept ourselves as more than just the physical image of our bodies. This connection allows us to recognize the wholeness within, and to reflect Truth and Love.

Truth always comes with peace, and reflects the true nature of compassion. It is very important for us to recognize our wholeness and the love that we have inside of us. This recognition is important before we attempt to share it, or give it away. So, if we do not recognize that we possess this Love of ourselves, how can we share it, or give this love away? This means if we don't love ourselves, we cannot share love—— only the illusion of love.

Compassion is the recognition of self-love. It is imperative that we recognize this love within ourselves for acceptance to take place. This allows us to recognize what it is we have to give. If we get only that tiny glimpse of what is to be seen (and yet tell ourselves that we understand), then what is it that we have to share or give away? Do we really understand what it is that we have to give away?

Clarity and understanding must come with compassion. This is where truth, peace and love reside. This is the natural state of Truth, when it is looked upon without judgment and fear. This natural state allows us to assess authentically what it is that we see. This is what is required in acceptance.

Our God and Creator have promised that the Truth will always be right in front of us, as a reflection of the universal Truth. The reality is, where else would the Truth be if <u>not</u> right in front of us?

Awareness is rather a general term. We are aware of many things that are going on around us all the time. Some examples of this awareness are the need for food, the air we breathe, and that feeling of being angry or sad. These are but a few of the thousands of things that are taking place around us every day.

However, most of us never really look at these events or situations with any level of understanding. We merely take them for granted. We say to ourselves that it is just there, and there is nothing we can do about it. But with this mode of thinking, we have forgotten that each event would not be what it is without our input, which makes it what it is. So, if we fail to discover or acknowledge this fact, we are led back to our lack of understanding, and to our poor perceptions. How often have we heard a person say they really don't know what happened, when they are the <u>source</u> of what happened? This speaks volumes to our lack of awareness of what is going on around us.

We need to understand that awareness gives us <u>choices</u>, and these choices give us our joy or our sadness, as a consequence of our decisions. It all depends on our level of acceptance. If we choose to be absent from an event, and tell ourselves we were not involved, are we conscious of our participation in what just happened? If so, there can be no discovery nor acceptance!

Understanding Our Choice

The cornerstone to our understanding and being aware is to recognize how our actions contribute to what we see, and the experiences we have. We must learn to not be afraid of our choices. By understanding our choices we accept that they have become a beacon to our clarity, and a honing device for our sound direction. But, it's also critical for us to acknowledge our <u>participation</u> in the situation. Often, we become angry or upset with little or no provocation over an event from our past. We then remove ourselves, as though we were not involved in the situation. We tell ourselves it is all about the other guys, and we had nothing to do with the outcome or circumstance of what just happened. When there is no acknowledgement of our participation, how can there be an awareness of our choices?

By embracing our choices, we have become aware of the growth that accompanies the process of our choices. This enables us to handle whatever comes our way: right or wrong, good or bad, we can always handle it. Then, we will be aware of our choices and can embrace them.

However, the denial of our choices keeps us confused and fearful about our direction, and this does not allow us to see our participation. This denial blinds us from our own choices. By acknowledging the choices we make, we accept the awareness to our spiritual connection.

Learning To Process

If we continue to allow our experiences to pass us by then how have we registered our participation? To process is to assess the clarity of any situation. To assess will lead us to look at what happened, and to register our involvement in the process. Assessment is not about judging the right or wrong of the events it is more about allowing ourselves the opportunity to get a clear picture of what just happened. Sometimes an event might be as far back as a month (or even a year), that we have never processed for clarity. This will leave an open-end situation that may require us to apply some form of clarity or understanding to have peace.

We harbor these feelings of confusion over an event from our past, which brought on displeasure with no clear resolution. These feelings and emotions will bring up old feelings of our own insecurity. And most of our insecurities stem from some unresolved issues of our past, either with ourselves or with others. To process is to look at these issues (whether they are painful or not), and to look at our participation, so we may become aware of what took place.

Hiding things or telling ourselves we have no clue as to how things got so bad is nothing more than a denial to our own involvement. We can never process without acknowledgement. Awareness is so broad a subject it would be hard to encase it into a small definition. But, more than anything, it is about discovery (or being fascinated) with the next moment. How can such a moment be defined with the limitations of our understanding?

Searching For The Truth

Our oneness starts with the <u>willingness</u> to see ourselves as complete and whole. When we can surrender to this way of thinking we will have given up the idea that we know the way. Oneness is beyond the idea that we know. It takes us to a totally different understanding by allowing us to recognize we don't need to know, we merely need to surrender to the knowing process, which is always continuous!

Our awareness is a critical part of surrendering to the truth. It requires us to give up the notion that we are in control. It removes the conflict and judgments from our thinking. When we are able to receive the experience without judgment we have allowed ourselves to take it all in. Then, we can experience the blessing of that moment. Our blessing will be a part of our every experience if we can learn how to surrender!

Awareness also introduces us to our inner-connectedness. This small part of us tells us that we are special and a major player in any situation or circumstance we face. This is the gift of that moment. By understanding this awareness, we become extremely focused and mindful of where we are, and who we are. Thus, Truth is revealed, right there in front of us!

Becoming Mindful

Being mindful is to recognize the clarity of our thoughts at any given moment. This is why it is so important to surrender and to let go of the limits we place upon ourselves. This can be difficult when we try to deny the presence of our own limitations. What is meant by this is that when we try to alter or change the Truth, we are in denial of what is in front of us.

We have all heard that meditation has been very helpful in letting go of some of the limitations we hold on to. There have been many meditation techniques passed on over the years which help us to free our minds, so we may touch our inner-self.

However, our continuous denial does not reflect any level of awareness or clarity of thought. But it does reflect fear and confusion. It is important that we take note to whether we are mindful of our daily lives or not. We must come to understand or realize that we can do more than merely be adrift on the sea of life, with no clear destination or purpose. It is important for us to understand our oneness, and what it means to be mindful, because this is what ties it all together for us. It helps us to bring about a clear understanding of what we are here to learn. This will bring us to a feeling of love and peace. This is the process of mindfulness.

Most of us interpret our lives in a very fragmented format. This fragmented form can only give us a limited understanding of our own stories. This becomes the means or methods to keep us confused and afraid. This method makes us take that small fragment and make it enormous, blinding us from our Truth.

A big part of becoming mindful is about recognizing our denials, and our need for control. It tells us to alter what we see. This will create illusions for us and have us accept this as our reality. It is telling us that we understand what we see, when (in reality) we understand only the small fragment of what it is we see. This is why it is important to become mindful: to be aware of what is going on around us, and to be conscious of the choices we have made. This will put us in touch with the experience itself, which is what brings forth the truth.

Every experience brings with it, its own blessing. This is the gift of that Holy Instant. With this mindful understanding, clarity is brought forth, as we experience that moment. Remember, peace is not something we can create, it is merely revealed to us. Only when we are in the right state of mind can it be recognized!

Clarity Of Our Thoughts

Clarity of thought is centered on recognizing the Truth and allowing ourselves to accept what is there. Often, in our desire to have a particular outcome, we deny what just happened. So, we may see what we want to see in front of us. However, when we see things this way, we have no clue as to what just happened. Remember, there are no coincidences in the process of acquiring clarity. Having this clear awareness will always provide for a sound direction to our choices.

Clarity is all about the recognition of the moment and what it brings (without the judgment of being right or wrong). It only requires a clear assessment of what happened. Clarity is not about a particular outcome, because clarity-of-thought can only come from that which has already happened.

Question: Have you ever thought about your best plan and how it turned out? As I look back on my own life. I realize that my own answer was not very promising. To think that I never had a plan turn out as I planned it, was amazing to me. The point here is that clarity is never about the past, or from our projections into tomorrow. It must (by its nature) reflect the moment, and this is always about the present or now and the Truth. We often just see it from the past, because time does not stop, so our images are from an event that has already occurred. Whether we like it are not, we made these choices....

Inner-Connectedness

When I asked my friends about the term "Inner-Connectedness", they told me many different understandings of what they believed it was supposed to represent or mean. One friend (who is a Buddhist), told me this approach speaks to the idea of reaching or becoming enlightened. This sounds like a truly meaningful method, to be able to touch our inner-self and feel connected to others. There are other friends that thought that it meant that you had to have received Christ in your life. This would allow you to have all your sins removed, and you would then be forgiven for all your past indiscretions. Science, on the other hand, recognizes that the universe is whole and complete, and it goes on to further state that there is only one universe. This implies that we must all be connected in some way, right?

When we take a close look at ourselves (from a place that carries no confinements, barriers or limitations), we will start to see ourselves as the "Godly Spirits" that we are! This will lead us to an understanding that we are all connected, and need only be aware of it, to accept it, as fact. In the book, <u>A</u> <u>Course</u> <u>In</u> <u>Miracles</u>, they speak of purity as not being contained (or restricted) by any barriers or limitations. This thought system was given to us so we may recognize that the body poses many limitations on us every day. This produces much confusion, because we can only see ourselves as a body, and this leads to conflict in the world. With this acknowledgement, we accept that we are greater than our bodies. This understanding will give us the freedom to see with a different vision: one that recognizes our Inner-Connectedness, and allows us to see our spiritual-self as one unit.

This new vision allows us to see the varieties of bodies, and still, recognize our oneness at the same time. This clarity and freedom will tear down the limits we have imposed on ourselves by removing the belief that we are in control. We can then realize that the experience is there to be cherished, and needs only to be appreciated for its clarity. This allows us to become aware of the freedom it possesses.

God (our Creator) is asking us to be aware of the simple statement that we are all connected. By recognizing this as the truth, we start to see with a new vision, which reflects our oneness! God's tasks are never complicated. We merely need to surrender to them and recognize their simplicity and clarity.

Better Understanding of Fear And Judgment

We need to look at fear and try to understand our confused state and our behavior over fear. President Franklin Roosevelt famously asserted, "The only thing we have to fear, is fear itself." This was, and is, a most profound statement that perhaps needs a bit of clarification. I think what was being stated was that fear is but an emotion that brings forth information both good and bad. Like all emotions, they need to be looked at for what it is they have to offer. This requires us to look at these emotions with the correct vision, so we may see the truth and clarity of what it is that they bring forth. This will allow us not to panic or be afraid of the information we have just received.

Judgment is defined as the ability to make a decision, or to form an opinion especially in matters affecting actions. The fear of being judged can bring on a loss of our ability to feel free within ourselves. The fear of being un-liked, un-wanted, un-attractive, or unworthy is sometimes too great to overcome. We are taught to nourish these fears and judgments by hiding who we really are, and this is often used to avoid our own embarrassment. We need to recognize that we do not need to be brave or courageous to function without fear or judgment. We only need to make a few small changes in how we see the world, and how we choose to interact with it, and with others.

Being Less Judgmental Frees Us From Being Judged.

Fear is but a signal of emotions given to us by our bodies. Fear is like many of the other emotions—it passes on basic information. A simple and useful definition of fear is stated by Dr. Albrecht: "An anxious feeling, caused by our anticipation of some imagined event or experience." Medical experts tell us that this anxious feeling that we get when we are afraid is a standardized biological reaction. In the publication "Psychology Today" (published on March 22, 2012 by Karl Albrecht Ph. D), Dr. Albrecht states that we are all afraid of the same few things.

When we look at some of our fears, we can all recognize that some of them are but basic survival instincts that we were given as a part our life. However, most of our fear is based from learned reflexes, and that makes us appear weak and fearful. These strange feelings of "fearing our fears" can be avoided if we learn to recognize them as being a message of clarity and understanding. They are but an instant reflex or reaction to our memories of our past fears. These reactions happen so fast we don't actually experience the fear itself; we experience a <u>short-cut</u> or <u>code</u> for this emotion.

This process keeps us trapped in the cycle of bad memories. This will have us fearing the memory of fear, even before it happens. It is like telling ourselves we are afraid of flying, even before we board the plane. So, is the fear actually about flying or is it about crashing? When we start to realize that fear is not an emotion that is harmful, but can be quite helpful, perhaps then we will see fear as a welcomed companion.

How does fear Work?

Fear can be a vital response to physical and emotional danger; if we did not feel it, we could not protect ourselves from a legitimate threat. Fear will often initiate the fight-or-flight response that is critical to any animal survival. According to science, the processing of fear takes place in our brain (in the subconscious mind) and cannot move outside of its fixed program. It is an automatic reaction to its previously stored behavioral responses. These responses work without our knowledge or our control. They are just our unconscious memories playing out our stored responses. This is why we generally are unaware of our behavior, according to Dr. Bruce Lipton, (a molecular biologist and former professor at Stanford University). In fact, he states that most of the time, we are <u>not</u> even aware that we are acting unconsciously.

Neuroscientists have shown that the conscious mind provides only 5% or less of our cognitive (conscious) activity during the day, and this is for only about 5% of us, who are consciously aware. He goes on to state that many people operate at just 1% consciousness. Dr. Lipton also says that the unconscious mind operates at 40 million bits of data per second, whereas the conscious mind processes only 40 bits per second. So, the unconscious mind is much more powerful than the conscious mind. It is the unconscious mind which shapes how we live our life. So, we must become conscious of being mindful and aware if we want to know who we are.

Fear is a chain reaction in the brain that often starts with some stressful stimulus and ends with the release of a chemical reaction that causes the racing of the hearts, rapid breathing, and energizes our muscle contractions, among many other things.

According to Dr. Karl Albrecht there are five basic fears that bring on all the other fears we face in our lives. He lists them as:

1. Extinction the fact or condition of being extinguished or extinct.

2. Mutilation to deprive a person or animal of a limb or other essential parts of their body.

3. Loss of Autonomy the loss of independence or freedom, or the loss of one's will or actions.

4. Separation the normal fear and apprehension expressed by infants when they are removed from their mothers (or approached by strangers), or any similar reaction in later life.

5. The Ego Death the act of dying; the end of life, an instance of death in the family.

The key factors in recognizing our fear is to notice the thought-system we are using to manufacture the fear. This happens when we can notice that strange sensations come up in situations or circumstances that are <u>not</u> familiar to us. We must learn how to navigate the many things in our lives (and in our social environment) that hold us hostage. With this recognition, we are able to let go of our old responses and change our patterns.

Most of our responses are just reflex-responses, which happen so fast that we are not really feeling the full effect of our fears. This is why it is possible for most of us to have those so-called "fear reactions." They are just memories of our fears revisited in our thoughts. The fear of height is a good example of this type of reaction, even when there is no need to fear it. It is like a child that is afraid of the shadows that are being reflected on the wall in his bedroom, from the tree outside the window.

Often, this is just encountering the memories of the past, or lacking the clarity of what it is we saw. Once we have processed those events of fears with our child, he will be able to approach his fears with a clearer understanding of what shadows are, and how to process them. Then, the shadows will disappear, like the illusion they are.

When we let go of the notion that <u>fear</u> is an <u>evil</u> force within us, we can begin to see that fear is just an <u>informative</u> source of basic information. We will then be able to recognize fear for what it really represents---- just more information about the experience. And this is <u>not</u> to be feared, but evaluated for its clarity and understanding.

Overcoming Our Fears

In overcoming fear it is important to learn what it is that we are afraid of. Many of the things we are afraid of are just our projections of uncertainty. This allows uncertainty to become a huge component in overcoming our fears. Learning to develop a better understanding of what frightens us goes a long way toward erasing our fears. It is also important to talk about our fears. This allows us to take in the experience and feel the sometime uncomfortable sensations in our bodies, and not to run away from them. This allows these experiences or sensations to feel less daunting, and not be so over-powering.

Seeking Help

Fear can be an overpowering emotion, and has been known to destroy lives. So, if we are having trouble in overcoming fear on our own, we should find a professional to help us. There are many treatments for fear out there, and there are some good resources that are available. With proper guidance from a trained professional, you can be helped.

Acceptance Of Self

Acceptance (or the loss of self-acceptance), can stem from our childhood. This is because there have been times in our lives when our parents have expressed a lack of acceptance of our "bad behavior." They told us this, and expressed it in many ways to note their disapproval. It is well-documented that our parents are more apt to tell us about our bad behavior (and how they disapprove), rather than expressing a level of reward for our positive attributes.

This approach has led to poor self-esteem and or self-criticism. The model that our parents have given us to follow will often be the one we will follow as adults. Most of us see ourselves as flawed, and this usually follows us our entire lives. We often learn to see ourselves without value, and not able to accept who we really are. We can only mirror the images that we were told, or given, as children.

The adverse effects of our parents' disapproval over the years has often created our bad behavior. Their constant expression that we are not smart enough, good enough, or worthy enough has resulted in most of us growing up and believing that we are only conditionally accepted. Most mental health professionals would agree that this is a subtle form of emotional abuse.

By our having to depend so much on our parents (or caregivers) when we were young, we became trained to believe what they told us about ourselves. Because we had little or no authority to question their actions, we just grew up with this mixed verdict as to what is the right approach. In many cases, we felt obliged to accept their negative appraisal as valid. This led us to believe that we were <u>unworthy</u> and <u>worthless</u> as beings. However, this berating approach did not stop with just our parents. It continued with our teachers, friends, siblings and others, adding to our lack of self-love and self-acceptance. This left us feeling alone and abandoned--thus creating the feeling of our separation. For true love to be expressed, we must be willing to surrender to <u>acceptance</u> as the process we use to take us there.

Self-Healing

<u>Self</u>-healing is a critical part of our recovery to loving ourselves, and this healing starts with surrendering to our spirits (despite

our short-comings). This would have been an automatic response had our parents and others not conveyed such a negative message to us. Self-healing is about acknowledging self, without judgment. This means to recognize that we are <u>complete</u> and <u>whole</u> as a spiritual being, and without the need or approval of anyone–for this is our birthright! We must rise to the challenge of accepting this as <u>fact</u> about ourselves, in order to start the healing process.

Many doctors now believe that a large number of diseases are caused by negative emotions, and that these emotions have been held onto for most of their patient's lives. These emotions (of hatred, fear, and anger or resentment) have built up inside, and have created diseases. In many cases, these patients are unable to accept themselves, or to release the bad thoughts they carry about themselves or others.

Self-healing is also about forgiving ourselves for those past discretions and the things we have assumed to be our fault. We must be willing to accept our new relationship of love with ourselves to find peace. In this process of acceptance of ourselves, we will find that happiness and compassion will become our new vision. We will come to realize that for most of our lives we have sought approval for our behavior from outside of ourselves (either from our parents or society in general). Seeking approval from outside of us did not allow us to recognize our true self. It is imperative that we go "inside" to make a connect with our unconscious spiritual self.

We must ask ourselves what it is that we don't accept in order to start the healing and to have compassion for ourselves. We can only do this through our loving understanding, and by accepting our imperfections as a part of our growth. Healing oneself is not just a physical act, but requires our mental and spiritual understandings, as well. So, as we heal our bodies, we must also recognize the need to heal our mental behavior (or spiritual self), as well.

More than anything else, we must become loving and compassionate to ourselves. Only then can we be loving and forgiving of ourselves. Only when we can grasp this understanding can we start to accept ourselves without judgment. Then we will start to realize that the picture we see is only the legacy of our authoritative parents, and not who we really are. We have all felt these conditional scars of our past. And yes, we have all been a part of our misguided caretaker's love. However, the key here is for us to recognize the injustices that have been passed on, and to make changes to our own attitudes. The real key is to change our approval seeking behavior so that we will be able to love ourselves.

Compassion

Compassion is a feeling that carries warmth and love, for oneself and others. It a very different feeling than empathy. You must feel a part of what the other person is feeling to have true compassion. True understanding of compassion is not just about seeing someone else suffer, and feel for them. This only reflects the understanding of the "word" compassion. To be compassionate, we must be willing to feel and experience it for ourselves, as a part of our own being, so we may receive all of the benefits from our connection. Then the act of compassion will be natural, because it will take no effort on our part for it to be shared.

We will feel this connection and it will become one with us. It is much like musicians learning a new piece of music. After a while, it all becomes natural for them. Their training and conditioning allows them to alter their brain patterns, to perform without thought or effort. This allows them to merely react to what is <u>now</u> natural.

Compassion is an act of kindness, or love, to oneself and to others. The more we practice this kindness the more it becomes natural, and the easier it is to share.

The Dalai Lama expresses it this way, "If you want <u>others</u> to be happy, practice compassion. If <u>you</u> want to be happy, practice compassion."

The key here is to <u>practice</u>. The tennis player needs to practice to become a great or a world-class athlete; we need to learn from them. Self-love is the most important key to seeing compassion. This is where we learn to be gentle and kind to ourselves. This means to recognize what is natural, and to see others as we see ourselves— with love.

Equality Of Compassion

This requires that we see ourselves and our brothers as one—— not in a physical way, but in a spiritual one. When can see beyond our bodies, and recognize that we are all sentient beings, we then feel connected. The interconnectedness is our ultimate purpose for being on this planet. To make this spiritual connection is to recognize our equality and the compassion that comes with it. When we can see the equality of our compassion, we will not focus on material possessions for that will no longer matter.

We must realize that suffering and hard times are but a process of transition. These experiences are not any less real; we all have hardship come our way. Even people with a great wealth have moments of hardship and suffering and need our love. We all have various levels of hardship. We must remember that compassion is not a statement of judgment–but a process of love.

There are many levels of transition, and when we can recognize this transition we will look upon our brothers and sisters with compassion. We will then know that the process of hardship and suffering will not last.

We have often been trapped by the thoughts or the idea of suffering. This has given way for us to feel pity for our brothers, rather than accepting their position as one of transition and a natural course of life. With this attitude of pity we will never be able to see our brothers as our equal.

Is Guilt A Process Of Destruction?

This is like asking if a mistake is a destructive process. All of us have made mistakes before, but the important thing for us to realize is that they do not define us. The book, <u>A</u> <u>Course</u> <u>in</u> <u>Miracles</u>, states that a mistake is only an <u>error</u> that needs our correction. When we apply corrections to any error it will usually disappear.

The only way that this does not happen is when we attach shame to the error or the mistake. Then we have labeled ourselves with something that we are not. Shame carries with it an attitude that we are not <u>worthy</u>, and that our mistakes reflect who we are. Guilt, on the other hand, merely tells us that a mistake has been made, and it needs our input to be corrected. Life reflects this example for every one of us, and does it all the time–this is called living! When we learn to accept this we will have made our <u>spiritual</u> <u>connection</u>, and will then be able to recognize our oneness. This will tell us that guilt is just a process that needs our attention.

The Unity Of Oneness

The nature of our oneness has been debated for centuries by philosophers and theologians. The discussions have always been to explore the conceivable theory and opinion about our <u>godliness</u>. I am not trying to tell you who God is; but merely telling you that the spirit of God (our Creator) is there inside of us and has always been there.

Regardless of your race, color, or language, or the religion you believe in, God has always been there–but often denied. However, to deny does not change the fact of God's presence; it only allows for us to believe that we know best. By using the approach of exercising our choice of free-will, we have found little or no peace from our guilt. Look at all the wars we have caused in the name of liberation, and yet, we continue to enslave ourselves and others.

How could this every be the choice of our Creator, if we are all connected as one?

God (our Creator) is love, and has only one direction, which does not leave room for alternate directions. This is the love our Creator speaks of, and wants us to see. Many people have told me about what they believe is a loving way, but when taking a closer look at what they said it does not reflect the oneness of love, at all. It merely expresses the idea of love.

The idea of love can only reflect mankind's way of seeing love, because it reflects many conditions and directions which are not those of love or unity.

The unity of our oneness allows us to see the spirit of our brother, and not just his physical self. This allows us to see the sentient being that he represents. Until we learn to recognize this being, we will only see the body— never to acknowledge the spirit of that sentient being that dwells within. Our acceptance always starts from self, and when we recognize our <u>own</u> spiritual-self, it will become easier to recognize others.

What do you think?

Thank you, much love.

REFERENCES

Ali, Abdullah Yusuf. *The Qur'An Translation*

Benedict, Ruth. *Patterns of Culture*

Boyle, Gregory. *Tattoos on the Heart, The Power of Boundless Compassion*

Byrne, Rhonda. *The Secret*

Brown, Laaren & Hort, Lenny. *Biography of Nelson Mandela*

Carnot, Sadi, In his 1824 publication of "Reflection on the Motive Power of Fire" In the article, he founded the Carnot's principle which today is known as second law of thermodynamics

Clarke, Arthur C. In his essay "Hazards of Prophecy: the failure of imagination ", *in profiles of the future 1962"*

Chopra, Deepak. *The Seven Spiritual Laws of Success. A practical guide to the fulfillment of your dreams*

Computer World, *November Issue, 2009*

Cobb, John Jr., and Griffen, David Ray. *Process Theology*

Coolidge, Olivia. *Gandhi*

Doa, Deng Tao. *Everyday Tao. Living with Balance and Harmony*

De Angellis, Barbara. *How Did I Get Here?*

Durant, Will. *The Story of Philosophy*

Durkheim, Emile. "Social control studied in the early 20th century"

Dychtwald, Ken. *Body Mind*

Eddy, Mary Baker. *Science and Health with key to the scriptures*

Gergen, Kenneth Jr. *The Saturated Self*

Gunaratana, Shante. *The 4 Foundations of Mindfulness in Plain English*

Harris, Sam. *The Moral Landscape, How Science Can Determine Human Values*

Hwa, Jou Tsung. *The Tao of Meditation Way to Enlightenment*

Hitchens, Christopher. *God is Not Great, How Religion Poisons Everything*

Hanh, Nhat Thich. *The Miracle of Mindfulness, A Manual on Meditation*

Johnson, Julian. *The Path of the Master, Radha Soami Satsang Beas Punjab, India*

Jones, Edmund Marc. *Gandhi Lives*

Jowett, Benjamin. *Six Great Dialogues: Apology, Crito, Phaedo, Phaedrus, Symposium, The Republic*

Kac, Mark. Professor at Cornell and Rockefeller University, states: "Probability is a cornerstone of all science and its daughter, the science of statistic"

Kelman, Herbert. Social influence in his paper, "The Journal of Conflict Resolution"

Kushner, Harold. *Who Needs God*

Kornfield, Jack. *The Wise Heart, A guide to the Universal Teachings of Buddhist Psychology*

Kellogg, Michael. *Three Questions We Never Stop Asking*

Keyes, Ken Jr. *Handbook to Higher Consciousness*

Kurzwell, Ray. *The Age of Spiritual Machines*

Lipton, Bruce. Bio… Social Consciousness.com

London Oxford University Press, The *Oxford Dictionary of Quotations, Second Edition*

Melchizedek, Drunvalo. *The Ancient Secret of the Flower of Life, Volume2*

Moyers, Bill. *Healing and the Mind*

Murphy, Joseph. *The Power of Your Subconscious Mind*

Myss, Caroline. *Anatomy of the Spirit, The seven stages of power and healing*

Oxford World Press. *Mahatma Gandhi, The Essential Writings*

Psychologytoday.com *Five Basic Fears We All Live With*

Pagels, Elaine. *Beyond Belief, The Secret Gospel of Thomas*

Rankine, William. The first thermodynamic textbook, in 1859, The first and second laws of thermodynamic emerged simultaneously (in the 1850's) primarily from the works of William Rankine, Rudoff Clausius, and William Thomson, 1st baron (Lord Kelvin)

Rasha. *Oneness*

Robinson, James M. *The Nag Hammadi Library, The Definitive Translation of the Gnostic Scriptures*

Renard, Gary R. *The Disappearance of the Universe*

Risner, Nigel. *The Impact Code*

Robert, Jane. *The Nature of Personal Reality*

Rumi. "The cure for pain is in the pain"

Simply Psychology, *What is Conformity?*

Smith, Bradford. *Meditation: the Inward Art*

Strachey, James. *Sigmund Freud, The Interpretation of Dreams*

Strobel, Lee. *The Case for Christ*

Taylor, Boltle Jill. *My Stroke of Insight*

Trungpa, Chogyam. *Cutting Through Spiritual Materialism*

TuTu, Desmond. *God is Not a Christian and Other Provocations*

Wallach, Wedell, and Allen, Colin. *The Moral Machine*

Walsch, Neale Donald. *Conversation with God, An Uncommon Dialogue*

Washington, James M. *The Essential Writing and Speeches of Martin Luther King Jr.*

Whitehead, Alfred North. *Process and Reality, Corrected Edition*

William, Mark, and Penman, Danny. *Mindfulness*

Williamson, Marianne. *A Return to Love,* Reflections on the principles of *A Course In Miracles*

Wikipedia. *Social Influence,* Turning, Alan. In his classic paper of 1950, "*Computing Machinery and Intelligence*"

Wikipedia. Nichelis, Miguel. Duke University Professor

www.ingramcontent.com/pod-product-compliance
Lightning Source LLC
Chambersburg PA
CBHW070632290526
45790CB00001B/80